A TRUE STORY

THE STORY TELLER

authorHOUSE

AuthorHouse™
1663 Liberty Drive
Bloomington, IN 47403
www.authorhouse.com
Phone: 833-262-8899

Published by AuthorHouse 05/25/2022

ISBN: 978-1-6655-6082-5 (sc)
ISBN: 978-1-6655-6083-2 (e)

Library of Congress Control Number: 2022910041

Print information available on the last page.

Any people depicted in stock imagery provided by Getty Images are models, and such images are being used for illustrative purposes only. Certain stock imagery © Getty Images.

This book is printed on acid-free paper.

CONTENTS

> I have been told through the years from many people
> that there are two, sometimes three, sides to every story.
> Even I have doubts about what happened sometimes, and
> I lived this life! But because there are many sides to me as
> well, I will give what I truly believed happened without
> betraying or dishonoring anyone mentioned. (All names
> have been changed to protect myself and those innocent
> and not-so-innocent people.)

> I don't remember too much about my first four years
> living in my birthplace of Northern California. So, I can't
> even go there. What I do know is we were a family once,
> with the two parents and the five kids. But I'd have to
> say by today's wording that we were dysfunctional. My
> mother was an alcoholic, so we wound up a single-parent
> family by the time I was one year old. My father single-
> handedly raised us the best he could with the help of a few
> ladies and their families. In 1959, my Dad got a job offer
> in Central Valley California driving big rigs. We moved,
> and this is where my story begins.

Alrighty now, I was done being the sweet little Paulo and I started on a path that is quite amazing. It started with my initial boxing career mentioned earlier. We (my brothers and I) eventually hit the circuit with our skills, boxing at Elks Clubs, American Legion Halls, and local boy's clubs. We would box each other or other boxers from around California.

The family moved from Central to Sacramena, CA and opened the California Boxing Gymnasium. I started training again and just partying a little on the side. I moved out at 16 years old and bought my first house at 18. By the time I turned 21, I held two amateur California State Golden Glove Championships. Professionally, I held a California State title and a North American Boxing Federation (NABF) title. I was also ranked #3 by the World Boxing Council (WBC) and #6 by the World Boxing Association (WBA). I was engaged to my first love and settling down.

My boxing license was taken away for illegal fighting, so at 22, I joined the Marine Corps to be a Sergeant. Within a few months I experienced the most horrific event that could happen to a young military man; I received a Dear John over the phone from my fiancé I was to marry in just one week. Within 10 months and 3 weeks, I transferred overseas and was honorably promoted to a corporal (E-4). In 1978, I was ranked a sergeant (E-5) in my beloved Marine Corps; it was a very proud moment in my life. When I got out of the Marine Corps, I went on a partying rampage. Somehow, I still managed to go to school and get Solar Utilization Certified, actually building and installing Solar systems. My first job was as a Pipe Fitter on Fort Ord.

These were the most turbulent years. I got back into boxing, won another California State title, moved onto drugs, biking, and partying with local motorcycle gangs, hunting, and fishing, all the while working. I feel I had a death wish; I didn't like people too much and knew I wouldn't make 40 doing what I was doing. 1990 was a big turning point in my life. At 35 years old, I was blessed with a three-day-old girl left at my doorstep who was my savior. For without her, I know I wouldn't have made 40.

I got married, off the drugs, divorced, and away from the entire bad, negative, no good people I had surrounded myself with, leaving me with a daughter to raise. It didn't take long before I divorced my wife who was on drugs and ran off with another man in drug rehab. Then my Dad had a stroke and I started running the gymnasium, raising Toni, and training Leroy. I got promoted and then discriminated against at the Printing Plant.

My Dad passed away and my relationship went with him. I took over the Gymnasium working 12-to-14-hour days and was still raising Toni. In my second marriage, we adopted Catherine and Louie, divorced in 1.5 years, I went back to college, and I took Salsa lessons.

By 2005 and through the first three years of living on 14th Avenue, I cut down an ugly-assed Palm tree, an even messier Black Walnut tree, a dying Oak tree, a weird-assed tree that dropped a lot of shit all over the place, and three very thorny lemon trees. I planted two Redwood trees I brought back from the Redwoods in the back yard, four white birch trees (two in the back and two in the front), three different types of palm trees in the front yard, two big ferns for the front porch area, and a nice weeping willow for the front yard. Every year I grow various tomato plants and keep my 16 different roses looking good.

Getting closer to retiring. Still have custom Harley and added a Harley Road King for longer rides. Joined Marine Corps League and Patriot Guard Riders. Get harassed at work some more then retire. I took up Tap dancing, did a recital then retired from Tap. Travel to Utah, Japan, Colorado, and then a Cruise. Niece is murdered by ex-husband. I meet sister and brother on my Mom's side for the first time. Single again and recruited by the United States Fight League to train their Athletic Inspectors. 2015 I have a significant emotional event on New Year's Day. I'm preparing to move to Hawaii in August. Once in Hawaii I feel right at home, starting fresh with only what I carried and acclimating to my new home...

MY SIDE OF THE STORY

INTRODUCTION

2004

I have been told through the years from many people that there are two, sometimes three, sides to every story. Even I have doubts about what happened sometimes, and I lived this life! But because there are many sides to me as well, I will give what I truly believed happened without betraying or dishonoring anyone mentioned. (All names have been changed to protect myself and those innocent and not-so-innocent people.)

The last ten months have been the worst I could ever have imagined. I was suicidal, homicidal, and at one time lost my mind for five complete days. During that time, I needed to get these feelings under control. A thought came from deep within me to write what had happened. I started voicing my thoughts on a tape recorder as I lay on the bed I used to share with my lovely, sensual, caring, beautiful wife. That made me feel better, hours passing as I was trying to make sense about what had transpired. Over and over in my mind I kept thinking about how betrayed I felt toward God and his concept of love. Why would I lose my wife, the son I adopted, and a good friend I had brought into my life five years earlier? I lost all of them in this 2003 Christmas season, a season I thought would be the best Christmas in my whole life, a Christmas I was going to make the best for all those under my roof. The thoughts of all the great times and the sexual encounters kept me loving and missing my wife. I was virtually dying inside.

So today, September 3, 2004, I started to write.

This is a biography of a man with several different names and, in the end, a completely new name. My current name, as listed on my California Driver's License is, Joe Paulo. I was born in 1955 in California to Valentino and Elaina. I wrote my story in seven-year increments, since most of the significant events have been during those years. I am the fifth and youngest child of Valentino and Elaina.

Living and growing up during the 1960s and '70s was a thrill that is unexplainable, especially in California, but I give it a try with some of my own recollections assisted by a few articles I've read explaining the '60s. The first is one of the best analogies of the '60s and it comes from George Carlin; if you can remember the '60s, then you weren't there. Truer words were never spoken. I feel very fortunate to have grown up during that time in America's history when the young adult population really seemed to make a difference, politically as well as artistically. I do realize how lucky I was to have lived, shared, and survived the "psychedelic experience."

My world was surrounded by the fast-paced world of sex, drugs, liquor, and the many types of music. And we loved every minute of it. From doobies, mushrooms, acid, mescaline, and booze, we experimented, and some lived through it all. Without condoning the use of drugs, I can vividly remember talking to trees (I still do at times), driving in our cars naked, swimming naked (sometimes still do that, too), walking down the street so stoned the sidewalk was visually coming up with my feet and swaying back and forth like a wave at 8:00 in the morning on the way to school.

I can remember the music of the Four Tops, Diana Ross and the Supremes, Motown, Jimi Hendrix, Janis Joplin, the Beatles, Santana, Malo, El Chicano, and so many more that helped shape my mind, body, and spirit.

We had concerts, riots, fights, a few deaths, and a whole lot of Lovin'.

Our friends and family were sent to Viet Nam in the world's most unpopular civil war action and many of them never returned; those that did were never the same.

We were a generation, perhaps the last one that shared a common bond through our music, our art, our literature, our heroes, our communal lifestyles, and, yes, our recreational mind-expansion. We spoke in a different common voice and, to the surprise of many, the world listened.

In the years that followed, many generations have tried to emulate the achievements and the fun history has proven to be so meaningful, but to no avail.

We had the Brown Beret (which I was a part of for a brief moment) and the Black Panther movements to keep things real, along with such heroes as John F. Kennedy, Martin Luther King, Jr., and Caesar Chavez (who I Marched with).

Everything back in the day was real and powerful to us, we believed we could make a difference and we did...

CHAPTER 1

1955-1962 (1-7 YEARS OLD)

INTRODUCTION

I don't remember too much about my first four years living in my birthplace of Northern California. So, I can't even go there. What I do know is we were a family once, with the two parents and the five kids. But I'd have to say by today's wording that we were dysfunctional. My mother was an alcoholic, so we wound up a single-parent family by the time I was one year old. My father single-handedly raised us the best he could with the help of a few ladies and their families. In 1959, my Dad got a job offer in Central Valley California driving big rigs. We moved, and this is where my story begins.

These were my only innocent years. I was a young four years old when we moved from Northern California to Central, California. The small town of Central had many characteristics to which I molded myself. The land was still raw and wild, just the kind of environment to grow up in.

1959

I grew up in Central Valley (or as we called it, Central) California. This is what it was like.

There is a place called Central Valley, California circa 1959-1968. To the east and across the Sacramento River is Sacramento. To the south and across the railroad track is WestSide. To the west is another small town called San Pedro. And to the north and again across the Sacramena River is what was once called Northern Light. Central is two miles in diameter and during the 1960s to early 1970s was a very small community with low-income yet clean homes. A kid growing up in Central didn't have to worry about going hungry since there were so many fruit trees and neighbors willing to feed a young kid with no mother. Being the youngest of five siblings, I got to learn from my brothers' mistakes and if I started problems, these brothers were there to straighten me out when they could, at least in the beginning. The town had a small police department, post office, and fire department. The schools, both elementary and junior high, were at the end of my block to the north. The store, fire department, post office, and swimming pool were at the other end of the block to the south. With the Sacramento River to the north and east we were always either swimming, fishing, frog gigging, hiking, camping out, hunting, riding our bicycles, or just hanging out at the river. I would have to say that every season was fun, but like most kids, the summers were more memorable. In winter, the fog surrounding Central was as thick as clam chowder. You couldn't see the hand in front of you, yet you knew where you were at all times. We would actually play hide and seek in the fog and hardly ever get caught. Every house seemed to have a fireplace and the aroma of wood burning in the winter was a welcome scent; it really made the place feel like home. The cold breezes could cut through your clothing like razors. Yet you always knew it wouldn't last long, since every house or destination was not that far away. The springtime was full of colors, purples, greens, oranges, and browns (even though I'm color blind I can still see colors); add in the different scents, such as fresh cut lawns, lilacs, Double Delight and Unforgettable roses, water on the cement, yet it was still as wonderful as the winter. Plus, you knew just around the corner that the fruits, cherries, nectarines, grapes, plums, Chinese cherries, oranges, and such a variety of apples, just to name a few, were about to ripen. The fishing was better as well. The summers were hot, but not too hot, since we always had the delta breezes. Autumn/Fall, whatever you wanted to call it, was sort of like a resting period for most of us. It meant we slowed down a bit and got our second wind while preparing for the winter. We wouldn't be outside as late but would still be out away from the house.

Many Central parents were very family-oriented in the sense that we could hang out at each other's homes, plus people didn't mind if a kid stayed overnight. They took care of each other by feeding and watching over us. I had a lot of surrogate parents or, should I say, role models growing up in Central. I have to say there were a couple of ladies who really stand out in my mind when I grew up in Central. They were Isabella and Millie, they treated me like their own son and to this day I still visit Isabella and her family. Yes, she still lives in the same house. As for Millie, I don't know what happened to her. Both would talk to me, check my homework after school, and invite me to their homes for parties, to eat, or just hang out. Since I didn't have a mother, they were just as kind, caring, and loving to me, which says a lot about their character. All in all, Central was the kind of place where everyone knew each other, and a guy or girl could walk down the street and not have to worry about getting hurt, except for this one asshole dog that lived at the corner. He was a shorthaired German Sheppard with a mean disposition. If I was riding on my bicycle, the asshole would chase me for blocks and half the time I didn't know if he was out or not. Sometimes it would be weeks with no sign of him, then boom! There he was on your ass trying to eat you. The one thing that finally got him locked up was when he chased and ate his last cat (which I think he hated more than me). He chased it down the street, around the corner, through one of those doors with the split top and bottom opening. He followed the cat through the top and into these people's house breaking everything he could until he caught the cat and ripped it apart. After that, he was always chained up in the backyard, never to be seen again, I was so relieved. Finally, I had my freedom to walk like a free man without being terrorized by the asshole.

When we first moved to Central, I was four years old. My sister Gina was the oldest, followed by Johnny the oldest son, then the twins, Nicolas and Nathanial. We were all 18 months apart. We had Spanish and Mescalero Apache blood which was evident by the twins' appearance, Nickolas looked more Apache; he was tall, dark-skinned, with straight black hair, and a quiet, gentle disposition. Nathanial looked more Spanish; he was shorter, light-skinned, damn near nappy black hair, and loved to get into fights. I never had so-called best friends except for that rare best friend Cesar who I knew and loved like a brother until the day he died in December 2006. Cesar flunked the first grade and was put into my class. We knew each other earlier; he sort of hung with my older brother

Nathanial. Cesar was Mexican and Yacque Indian, short, chubby, had a big nose like a shark fin, and wiry, damn near nappy hair too. We had all kinds of names for him like the Great Pampero (after a local wrestler), Assadami Steve., and Foolio. (I'll remember a few more later.) Cesar's Mom (Doris) was very nice to me, but to Cesar, she was very strict. Mainly because Cesar was the youngest and was a lot like his Dad when his Dad was younger, Cesar had a mean streak and a knack for getting into shit. One-time Cesar pissed off Doris, so she pulled off a piece of the wood paneling strip and started to beat Cesar with it. I walked very calmly yet swiftly out of the house. Man, did Cesar get his ass whipped that time. Cesar's Dad (Bennie) was the coolest Dad around. If Cesar got in trouble, his Dad would want to hear the whole story. It was like he was reliving his past. He wouldn't tell Cesario (as he called him) how to do it right the next time he would just smile and listen. He especially liked to hear about the fights and about the girls we would be with. (That, my friend, I will have to tell you about when we get to the next seven years and beyond). Cesar was the funniest guy I ever met, he would tell jokes and stories all the time. All stupid incidents that occurred and he had a knack for making them all the more stupider.

There was a girl named Mary, and we were in kindergarten when we first met. She had the prettiest golden blond hair with curls like a slinky toy. One would best describe her as a Shirley Temple look-a-like. Her face was as white and round as a marshmallow. Mary lived in a corner house around the corner from me. We were inseparable for months. Mary's mom was so kind and soft-spoken; she really made me feel at home when I was there. Mary's mom would bake cookies for us and make sandwiches and stuff while Mary and I would play in their backyard. Mary's mom never let us out of her sight. To this day, it really makes me wonder what she was afraid of, especially since all of a sudden, one Saturday morning, I went to Mary's to play, and they were gone. All their furniture, outside stuff, and toys were gone. I think, or should I say assume, they were running from someone. I hope it wasn't an estranged husband or a person that meant them harm. I don't know what had happened to them; all I know is that I was introduced to my first broken heart at a young age of five.

After Mary, I hung around with another girl, Terri. Terri was taller than me and very strong; she was a cute tomboy. Terri lived on the same block as I did, only on the opposite north side and on the corner. Terri's mother was another single parent and was just as kind to me as Mary's mom. Their family was from Oklahoma and they had this very thick Okie accent. I could sit and listen to them talk for hours; you know Okies always had a story to say about anything. I do miss their fried chicken, biscuits, mashed potatoes, and gravy. Terri would come to my house on her bicycle, grab me by the shirt, kidnap me, and take me to her house to play. My brothers teased me, but I didn't care. Terri was so cute, with her accent and all; on top of that she fed me!

At five, I was in my first car wreck. I was in the front passenger seat with my Dad in our old Hudson Station wagon. We were driving north on fifth Street and as we were going through the intersection of fifth and I Streets, an old couple ran the red light and we ran into them, they were driving a big new Cadillac. I hit my face on the steel dashboard just under my nose and across my gums. My nose was bleeding and my face swelled up, but it looked worse than it was. The old couple knew they were in the wrong and seemed really sorry for the accident. The ambulance gave me the once over and cleaned me up and had me take a few aspirins and some ice to ease the swelling. I believe the couple paid off my Dad later and we were alright with that.

My initial boxing career started at seven years old, and it seems every day at 6:00 p.m. my brothers, my sister, and I would train as boxers. The garage was converted into a little gym filled with two heavy bags, one two-ended-bag, a speed bag, and mirrors. We also utilized the two patios; one was next to the garage and the other was next to the house for shadow boxing and jump rope exercises. I loved the idea of beating on the heavy bag and watching it fly all over the place as I would calculate its movements and get in position to beat it some more. It was one of those things I used to get in trouble for when I would do the same thing with the pillows in our bedroom. I would fly from one bunk bed to the other, slugging the pillows back across the beds, then jumping on them and slugging them to the next bed. Man was that fun and good exercise, too! I would say I took to the training like a duck to water. My Dad would have us spar with each other, and sometimes we'd have the whole neighborhood come over to spar or let them spar each other. It was funny how Dad would see one of our friends and size him up really quick and before you know it we'd be matched up, gloved up, and sparring before they could say a thing. After a while, some of the guys quit coming over, knowing that if they did, they'd be matched up and boxing.

Then it happened, I got my first piece of ass at 8 years old…

CHAPTER 2

1963-1969 (8-14 YEARS OLD)

INTRODUCTION

1963

Alrighty now, I was done being the sweet little Paulo and I started on a path that is quite amazing.

It started with my initial boxing career mentioned earlier. We (my brothers and I) eventually hit the circuit with our skills; boxing at Elks Clubs, American Legion Halls, and local boy's clubs. We would box each other or other boxers from around California. After each bout, the patrons would throw money into the ring and we would collect and split it between the two fighters. I had two very good paydays (making over $48 each time). One was in the Elks Club at the old Elks Building off J Street, with a world champion's little brother. He was a little bigger than me and had more boxing experience than me, but I didn't care (neither did my dad), so we fought it out very hard and fast. I was an animal! I just kept coming and hitting. He boxed (hit and move), I was very aggressive, and it ended up a close decision, but they gave it to him. The crowd was wild throughout the whole bout; afterward they showed their appreciation by throwing over $100 worth of change and dollar bills into the ring. That was a good boxing lesson he demonstrated, and it showed I had a lot of heart, determination, and meanness. The next one was with my brother Nathanial at a Sickle Cell Anemia fundraiser at the McClellan Air Force

Base auditorium. Nathanial was bigger and stronger than I was, and we were supposed to put on a demonstration and just spar lightly. The next thing you know, Nathanial snuck in a hard combination that stunned me! I went off and attacked him with amazing speed, strength, and perfect accuracy that he was knocked through the ropes and onto a spectator's lap. The crowd went wild! My dad acted like he was mad at us, but I think he was a very proud man that night. Nathanial showed a nice combo, and they all learned I possessed a lot of power and inner strength when needed. We received $48 each for our performance!

At eight years old, I had my first piece of young ass…

Her name was Christine; she was a Portuguese tomboy if there ever was one. Christine would hang out with my brother Nicolas and me; that meant she would go to the river with us to fish or swim, or we'd go hiking and shine shoes downtown then use that money to go to the movies and just hang out. The swimming part is what got me started with her because she would just have a tee shirt and shorts on. You could see right through the tee shirt and those young perky little nipples would just turn me the fuck on. I would guess she knew that so one time she caught me stealing a cigar from a neighbor's car and threatened to tell on me if I didn't do something for her, or should I say, to her. Ya know I had to say, "OK" or else I wouldn't be telling you this story. Christine had me follow her behind some bushes next to a fence. She politely asked me to take my pants off while she was taking off hers. She had me lay my shirt on the ground, so she could lie on it. I saw her cooter and it was small and smooth. Christine saw I was already aroused and ready to do something with this hard-on, so she told me to put it in the spot. I'm looking at the cooter and thinking, I'm too big for the little cooter, so I told her this. She told me it stretches open. So, I tried to get it in, but it was too dry, so I licked my hand and moistened the cooter up a little, which Christine liked. Finally, I got it in and (Dammit! I'm getting a hard-on just telling the story!). OK, OK, I'm focused again. When I finally got it in, I felt this warm rush come over my whole body, and it was all illuminating from down there. I really don't know whether she came or not, all I know is I was hooked on the feeling and would need to get it back again soon. Christine and I did the thing quite often after that until she let the word get out and her brother Raul told their Mom about it. So, there we were, Christine and her oldest sister Janey to my right, with Raul to my left, all of us standing in front of their mom. Their mom was a very big, menacing woman. She was so big (probably 350-400 pounds, maybe bigger!) that she was bed ridden and never got out of the bed that I know of. Either way, she told us about what she heard and asked if it was true. I wasn't about to lie to this woman, even though Christine did, I said it was true and got away with only a very stern warning from her. Christine on the other hand got her ass beaten for lying and was put on restriction. That, my friend, was the last time we did it for a while. But it didn't stop me from looking for it elsewhere. There were other girls in Central that liked to do the wild thing at our young age, too. I happened to track down a couple of them in sisters named Janet and Dina. One was tall and skinny and the other was short and chubby; both were party girls who loved to give head and fuck. We would go to the river, in the surrounding fields, the baseball dugouts, or wherever we could to have a little fun. This lasted a couple of years and I started finding other girls that wanted some cock.

Then there were the girls I dated that didn't give it up so easily. Elsie and I were 11 years old when we dated in the sixth grade. Elsie was a very beautiful girl who was ½ Philipina and ½ Spanish. Elsie was very short (under 5') and had very long, straight, dark brown hair past her butt. Elsie was dark-skinned with freckles and a body that was straight up and down, no girly shape at all. It was her face, her soft voice, and her long hair that grabbed my attention, not to mention her beautiful naturally red lips. Elsie had a very quiet, soothing effect on me. I would say she was my first crush and one of the very few I ever dated and never did anything sexually with. I still have a crush on her. I saw her once, after I got out of the Marine Corps. I was just driving around the old neighborhood and saw her in front of her old house on Black Beards Drive and I stopped and talked to her. I could not believe my luck! She was even more beautiful than ever, she filled out and her body had curves to it that gave me an instant hard-on. Her hair was shorter but still long. We talked about our past and actually made out in her front yard for a minute. I wanted to start seeing her again and start dating but she kind of stopped there and reminded me that she couldn't have babies and that I would probably want them one day. I think she might have already been in a relationship and wanted to make excuses for not wanting to begin another one with me. I tried to talk her into reconsidering, but it didn't work, and we left each other all moist and alone. I still have a crush on her and drive by her old house from time to time. I never see her, though.

Then there was Eileen, a beautiful African-American with a body that was to die for. She was as tall as me and had short nappy hair with big lips and well…let me start on this body of hers. At 12 years old she was already developed in the upper and lower parts. Eileen was big breasted with a very small waist (23") and a big butt! Yet, she was firm too! Eileen was another girl I dated whom I never slept with. Eileen's family was all into music. Barry, Ellis, Norma, and Linnie all played musical instruments and sang. As a matter of fact, the whole family could sing and play. Eileen and I were better at being best friends than being girlfriend and boyfriend, so we decided to break up and be friends. I see her at her Brother Ellis's funeral in or around 2001; she looked beautiful and quite mature. At Ellis's funeral, she sang and her voice was magnificent. She married Ebenezer and they moved to Kansas where Ebenezer was working as a Correctional Officer in Leavenworth State Correctional Facility. Growing up in Central, Eileen's family was like a second family to me along with my next girlfriend.

Janine (13 years old) was another beautiful African-American. Janine had a big natural (Afro), a very slim body with all the right curves and a beautiful smile, with such a soft voice that I could barely hear her at times. Janine also had very soft, light-colored skin I loved to touch. Her brother Joseph and I were like brothers; we hung out together all the time, which made Janine a little jealous at times, but since Joseph was her little brother, she didn't mind too often. I got my first piece of ass off Janine at our eighth-grade graduation party. After that we were getting busy all the time. Janine's mom loved me and kept telling me that she wanted me to be her son one day. I would have loved to be at the time since Janine and I were such good friends and lovers. Plus, I loved her whole family and they loved me. Eventually, we grew apart just before I moved from Central, but we remained close friends and continued communicating even after I joined the Marine Corps. Janine eventually married and had a couple of girls and moved out of Central. I caught up with her in 2005; we went out for a few drinks and dinner by the river, then for a walk and a few more drinks in Old Sacramena. When we finally got back to her Mom's house we made out in the driveway like we used to back in the day, plus we felt each other up and down just because. We both said we loved each other and to keep in touch. I've never seen her since. I need to say, her brother (our brother) Joseph died at a very early age (20s). The story was he was drinking and slipped next to a pool at an apartment complex in Central and fell in and drowned. Another story was that he got caught with another man's woman and got knocked out from behind and thrown into the pool and drowned. It was a great loss to all of us; our Mom never recovered from the tragedy, nor did the rest of us in our own way.

1964

Nine years old and getting caught stealing by neighbors…

Our neighbors were Redneck Hillbillies, every one of them! They ran around their pee-smelling house in their underwear or panties and bras. The house was a mess all the time. So, one day I was over there and waiting for one of the girls to come out from the back room and I decided to check a few drawers out. Well, I happened to find a pile of silver dollars in the drawer and decide to take a few ($10). Later that day I was called back to the house by Eva (Mom #2) and the mom and grandmother of the hillbillies. The Hillbillies wanted me to strip naked so they can see that I didn't have the money hidden on me. Eva refused to let this happen and decided to wait until my dad got home to handle the situation. My dad had a way of getting things out of me; I think it was the fear of getting beaten if I lied, so I told him the silver dollars were hidden around the corner. He decided to go with me to find the money. We walked around for blocks; it was a nice warm evening and with the Central breeze, it ended up a nice walk I had with my dad; we never did that before. Well, after a while and me not knowing what to do, he stopped and asked me again, where's the money at? I came clean and told him it was at home under my mattress. We gave the money back to the hillbillies and I was never allowed back into their house again.

1965

Ten years old and smoking my first joint with Ricky was a trip! I don't know where we got the big-assed Cheech and Chong joint but we had it and we smoked it! I don't know what happened afterwards. All I do know is we were at my house lying on the front room couch when we heard the doorbell ring and all we could do was look around from our dazed heads and wonder where the noise was coming from. After a few more rings we got our heads straightened enough to hear Sammy at the front door yelling at us to get the fuck up! We told him what we did, and he just laughed at us and asked how we felt? What a dumb question, it was all over our face that we were in a stupid state of mind!

I was only 10 years old when I broke into Deerhorn Elementary school with an older guy (14 years old). We wrote nasty stuff about the teachers and the principal. We then broke 27 windows and trashed a few classrooms before deciding to take a break in the teachers' lounge and eat some cookies and drink a few sodas. It was on the way back to our bicycles that we got caught by the local police. The dude I was with started crying like a big-assed baby about how his mama was going to beat his ass and how much trouble he was going to be in. I got pissed at the big crybaby and told him to shut-up and that I was going to get into as much trouble and that my dad would beat me even worse. I even asked the cops to let me out of the car because I didn't want to be next to the crybaby. They told us both to shut up! It just so happened my dad was more disappointed with me than anything. I didn't even get an ass whooping. I went to court and luckily, the judge knew my dad from the boxing matches in town and just made me work off the damage.

That was when I started working for Ms. Campbell; she was the school janitor. Ms. Campbell was a short heavy-set older white woman. She liked me and sort of took me under her wing. There was another guy from the court system working off his sentence, too. He was a stocky, long blonde haired, handsome white kid, a little older than me, too. He was lazy and Ms. Campbell didn't like him too much. I worked hard for Ms. Campbell, and from time to time she would show me how to do more important things like working the buffer or painting the walls. I liked her a lot! After the summer was over and my time was through, Ms. Campbell hired me on as a part-time employee; it was my first official job. She even started taking me home at lunchtime and feeding me and introduced me to her mother, another old white lady. Then she started having me save money in a little piggy bank she bought me. When the piggy bank got too small for the cash, we opened a bank account at the Bank of America. She definitely was a blessing to me; I really liked her and her mom. I've been by her old place next to the Sacramento River a few times. There's a boat ramp across from her old place and the house is still there looking as old and wore out as before.

1966

Eleven years old and I was a solid drinker whose taste for wine and beer was getting worse. I even tried smoking cigarettes for a few months; they are just too nasty and only made me dizzy and stinky. I had just bought my first pocket knife from Sprouse Ritz store. So I was walking home when a girl who was a bully and stood taller than me, was heavier than me, and older, started to bully me around. So, I pulled out my new clean knife and started to stab her. She was waving a bag she had in her hand at me and I got a few stabs at her hand and arm. She ran home and a few hours later the cops were at my doorstep. I explained what had happened and how she always bullied people. They dropped the charges and took my knife and figured it was self-defense. I'm guessing she had priors. She never bothered me again and the word got out in this small town that I would stab someone if need be!

My brothers and I, along with our friends, would camp along the river or build forts and have battles. The most fun we had was at the old cement plant. The pond (which we called the Cement Pond) was full of old cement wastewater, pollywogs, and frogs. That is where the real battles were fought. We would build rafts and cross the cement pond to meet in the middle and have the battle for supremacy of the Pond. Another very traditional treat was Tightwad Hill. It was next to the Speedway Racetrack a few miles west in the Westside side of town. Tightwad Hill was on the levee next to the railroad tracks. We could see all but the north side of the tracks. We would usually go there for the drugs, drinking, and girls. Occasionally, we would actually pay and go into the Racetrack, but not too often (it wasn't as much fun).

A friend of mine was Cesar; he liked to fight and every time his nose would bleed like a water fountain. He was tough, yet stupid for fighting because he really couldn't fight that good, even though he did win sometimes. So between the bleeding and the ass whooping he took, I really couldn't see why he would even go there. I always had his back, though; I would stop it once it got too bloody or he was getting his ass kicked too badly and didn't want to stop. He was a fair fighter. I remember Ricky (Mister Five Finger Discount) tried to give him a bottle when he was getting a boxing lesson from one of the better street fighters in the neighborhood and Cesar turned it down and well, I had to stop it. The damn fool, he just wouldn't give up, and it was over a chick who was cheating on another one of our friends (Chuy). Now, how stupid is that? The following day Chuy saw the guy in the boy's restroom and went in to kick his ass. The other guy came walking out in less than a minute and we went in to find Chuy knocked the fuck out. We started laughing because Chuy couldn't fight either, as a matter of fact; Chuy was way less of a fighter than Cesar.

Then there was Ricky, called Mister Five Finger Discount because he could steal just about anything he put his mind to. Ricky was a light-skinned Mexican with big round ears. I witnessed him walking out of Bruner's with a $1500 Persian rug, all rolled up and heavy. He just walked out of the store with it. When I asked him how he did it, he just said, these people wouldn't think a kid would just walk out of a store like Bruner's with a Persian rug. Did I mention, he was only 12 years old and we skipped school to witness it? (OK, I should not get ahead of myself.) Yea, Ricky had nuts like Penitentiary Steel. He ended up putting this Persian rug in his garage, that's where his bedroom was. His stepdad didn't like him too much since he lied most of the time and stole the rest of the time. His room was not that bad, though; he could come and go as he pleased and have friends over anytime. He stocked it with the best his little hands could steal, and his stepdad didn't ask any questions.

Ricardo (Chita) was half Filipino and half White on his mom's side. Chita was short, sort of stocky built, and didn't laugh; he cackled with kinda nasty bucked teeth. Chita was a great guy to hang out with because he would do anything he felt like doing. Plus, he had two of the most beautiful older sisters in all of Central. My goodness, just thinking of them reminds me of the memorable evening when Chita and I were sleeping in the front room and, in the middle of the night, his sisters got hungry and went into the kitchen to get some snacks. I acted like I was asleep, and man did I get an eye full of half-naked teenagers with only their panties and bras on. Dammit, I can still see them as if it were last night. Do you know what a vision like that can do to a seven-year-old kid? I was in love with them sisters forever more. Chita's mom was fun too; Chita would piss her off so bad that she would start chasing and hollering at him until her false teeth fell out. We would almost pee on ourselves from laughing so hard. She could never catch him either. Chita's dad was one of the nicest dads too. He was a full-blooded Filipino and had the heavy accent, too. He had to sleep most of the day because he worked graveyard shift at Campbell Soup Company. Chita would crawl on his hands and knees into his dad's room and steal money, so we could by junk or do stuff. Almost every time Chita would get caught as he closed the door, but it was too late, we would run from the house while Chita's dad would be hollering, Chita! Chita! We would just keep running and never got caught.

Around the same time, I had my first crack at sniffing paint with a few of the boys. We would gather at the baseball diamonds next to Raley's store, huddle in the dugout and get stoned! My biggest trip was when Ricky and I were sniffing. We were tripping hard and heavy because I heard Ricky screaming and when I looked at him, a big, white mean rabbit with long nails and teeth was on his back biting and scratching him! I started slugging and pulling the rabbit off Ricky until it disappeared. We looked at each other and I looked at his back and the scratch marks disappeared, too! Then we looked at the pitcher's mound and the rabbit was sitting on its two back paws as a big dark cloud started coming over the baseball diamond. Ricky and I looked at each other again and yelled, "run!" We ran out of the dugout, cleared the diamond then stopped across the road and watched as the cloud covered the diamond and the rabbit disappeared again. We never ever talked about the incident after that.

My brothers Nicolas and Nathanial and a few of us guys started working at the Woodbine Tomato fields. We would walk from our house, picking up a few of the guys and stopping at certain houses that had the Crystal Milk Home Delivery, and we would take some cheese from one house, sandwich meat from another, mayo from another and add that to the bread we already had and walk toward Old Sacramena by way of the lower train level of the "I" street bridge (The Black Bridge). Old Sacramena back in the '60s was actually Skid Row. Bums lived in the old abandoned building and winos lay on the sidewalks. We would be out there before 5:00 am to catch a bus to Woodbine. Working in the tomato fields was a trip! The Mexican workers didn't speak English, and we didn't speak Mexican. They didn't like us too much and a few times we got into fights with the younger ones. Once I was eating one of my stolen sandwiches and a Mexican kid came up (with the urging from older Mexicans) and started a fight with me. I jumped up and started raining punches down all over his stupid ass. I guess they must have had bets on him and since he lost, so did I; they fired me and told me I had to leave for starting a fight, bummer. Walking home from the tomato field all dirty and stinky was sort of embarrassing at times but worth the extra money we received, which was 25 cents per crate.

My next job was at Flava's Grocery store, stocking the shelves and cleaning up the place. Flava's was a very small store and making 25 cents an hour was not a lot, but I did get to eat a certain amount of goods for free. And after a while, I was able to learn how to steal beer from the back cooler with the help of a few friends. So, it all worked out for my pals and me, especially since the owner was a prick!

My brother Nathanial and I started mowing or raking lawns for extra cash, too. We would even climb up trees and cut mistletoe down and sell it during holidays. We had a lot of practice raking leaves since our dad would have us up and raking our yard every Saturday morning while he supervised us; we got pretty good at it. Our customers had us come back we were so good! Some of the boys and girls and I would skip school and hang out at one or another's house and get blue balls with the girls or get lucky. We would hang at the house that had no parents home to disturb us. Sometimes we would buy wine or beer and drink and party; other times we would just make out and get busy. The thing I remember the most about these encounters is the music of the '60s. The Motown, Psychedelic, or '50s oldies was the music we loved, danced, and sang to back then. We would sometimes hang downtown stealing and messing around there. We also did nice things like go to the movies. We would collect enough money to get one person in and that person would open the back-alley door for the rest of us and we would watch a movie. One time during the summer, we were waiting at the back-door sweating and blinded by the sun. When we were let in it was so dark that I couldn't see for the life of me and I ran into a big pillar next to the emergency entrance to the show. I heard a lot of laughter only to find out that just about everybody in the show saw me hit the pillar and fall on my ass and crawl to the closest seat I could find. When I got my sight back I was looking around and started to laugh at myself for being in such a hurry and running into the pillar. I ended up with a nice knot on my forehead too.

There were two times I almost drowned in the Sacramento River. Once was when the family and my dad and his friends were at the Northwest side of the river. My dad was relaxing with some of his friends and didn't notice that when I swung out too far into the river off the rope that I hit an undercurrent and was drowning. My sister Gina saw me sinking and waving my arms for help and swam out and saved me. We didn't say anything to my dad because then I wouldn't be able to swim anymore. She made sure I didn't go too far out again either.

The second time I almost drowned was at the Northeast side across from what is now Old Sacramena. I was with my brother Nicolas and Christine. We were swimming off the docks by the Black Bridge. Usually we would swim across the river to the Sacramena side and back just because. Well, this one-time Christine and I both got sucked under by an undertow. Nicolas tried to save us, and we almost drowned him. Luckily, there were a few grownups in a boat leaving the docks, and they were able to grab our little asses out of the water and save us. I keep remembering the light as I kept swimming to the top of the water and then the way it kept getting darker and darker as the undertow kept pulling me back down. This happened a few times. I tell you what, we sure were lucky to be saved that day. Many friends have drowned in that stretch of water over the years.

1967

Twelve years old and trying hallucinatory drugs such as acid, mescaline, and mushrooms, was the thing to do back then. We would do this during the weekday, weekend, or anytime we felt the urge. Especially on the weekends when we had more time to discover ourselves, plus the girls loved the stuff too! There we would be in mixed company of kids and parents and they wouldn't even know that we were tripping something terrible or mellow, depending on the drug. I can still remember walking through

Cesar's house during the daytime and his parents were watching TV and when I passed them by, I looked at the TV and all I saw was that fuzzy stuff like when the TV is off for the night. You'd have to be older to remember the TV broadcasting stopped at a certain time of the evening. It wouldn't stay on all night like they do now and an electrical tower with a bolt of electricity would run through the tower signaling no power.

Two of my best street fights were against two bullies from Central, both white boys. One was Bob; he was a big white boy. Cesar and I were hanging out at the California High School parking lot after the basketball game when we saw Bob chasing this smaller Mexican kid and his girlfriend through the walking trail in front of the school. He finally caught up with them in the parking lot. Bob started pushing around the kid while the kid's girlfriend was watching and looking very scared. Bob had a couple of friends with him, too. Cesar and I ran over there, and I pushed Bob and told him to back off, the kid didn't want to fight. Bob told me it was none of my business and told me to back off, he didn't want no trouble with me. It was between him and the kid. I insisted he back off! Bob took a swing at me and then bum rushed me. I caught him with a nice jab and started to give him a good old boxing lesson. Straight up, we got into it a little and then it happened. He kneed me in the nuts and I immediately grabbed him by the throat or should I say the windpipe. Then I had him in a position he couldn't get out of. I already had a bruised right knuckle from an earlier incident and didn't want to hit him too much with it but did anyway. As I was fighting him, Cesar was keeping the other guys back, so they didn't jump in, they just watched as I tore into their buddy. I had to switch hands and when I did, Bob started to fall. I got a good grip on his throat again and started to beat him with my left hand. When I finished, I let him go. He was barely leaning against the car he got beat on when Cesar went up to him and said, "fight my friend with his bad hand will you?!" And Cesar slugged him in the face and knocked him down for the count. By this time, a lot of people were there from the basketball game and Big George told Cesar he was chicken shit for hitting Bob after I already beat him. Cesar got in Big George's face and told him about my hand and how the fight got started in the first place. Big George didn't care and neither did Cesar and they almost got into it before someone yelled the teachers were coming, so we split the scene. The next day at school the word got out they were going to jump Cesar, so I made sure the word got out that it would not be a good idea. The day was tense but uneventful.

The other kid was JohnBoy. JohnBoy was small like me and a mean little redhead asshole. He already had a reputation for kicking ass and everybody believed he was the baddest. I didn't think he was so bad. As a matter of fact, I thought he was all talk. So, one day, Sammy, Cesar, and I were walking by the Dairy (the Dairy was a small corner drive-thru, a 7-11 type of place) and JohnBoy said something stupid to one of us and I called him on it. He told me he wasn't talking to me and it was none of my business. I squared up on him and told him I was making it my business. The dumb ass bum rushed me and pinned me against a fence. I started laying down some body shots and he had to let go. As we were squared off, I saw he had that scared look in his eyes and said he didn't want to fight. I told him he was a pussy and he was supposed to be so tough let's do this. He started to bum rush me again and I went street on him and Sammy told me to box him. I preferred to just beat him down at his game and it worked. The next thing you know, he was backing down and away all bloodied and bruised saying he didn't want to fight anymore. I kept stalking him into the Dairy drive-thru and stopped long enough to tell him that he best stays away from us and to stop picking on people he knows nothing about. The word got out that I could street fight besides box and I had no trouble after that. Not that I had trouble before; it's just easier when people respect you for helping people than when you are a bully.

I enjoyed venturing out of Central every now and then, especially riding our bicycles to the State Fair on Stockton Blvd and Broadway sneaking in through a hole in the fence seeing BB King, Paul Revere and the Raiders, the Go-Go Girls in cages, and a lot of fine chicks in hot pants and bikini shorts (Who would of thought we would eventually be living just down the street from the fairgrounds in the near future?).

1968

At the age of 13, my family moved out of Central and into Sacramena's Tahoe Park area. It was a whole new world moving from Central to the big city. Tahoe Park was across the street from Oak Park. Both were different in the sense that Oak Park was home to the Black Panthers, a racially active group much like the Chicanos' "Brown Berets," with which I was affiliated back in the day. In Central, every race got along, but in Sacramena, every race fought each other. I didn't understand it at first; but I found out real quick why and kept to myself for a long time. I was not into all the bullshit. Tahoe Park was full of trees and, since we lived off of a main street (Stockton Blvd.), just as many cars. All the colors and scents were different and I couldn't quite get in tune with my surroundings; it just wasn't the same. The schools were walking distance but still hard to understand with all the tension. I decided to do my own thing and work, train (boxing), and go to school when I had to. Living in Tahoe Park was very different for me and at 14 years old, with a lot of time on my hands, I got into a lot of good and bad things. On the one hand, I got into drugs, drinking, women, and street fighting again.

On the other hand, I got into boxing, working out, and trying to find the better of the two and get away from it all, especially after seeing these young beautiful Chicanas all doped up and just out of control; it made them look so ugly and cheap! One Chicana named Rosa was so fine and easy to talk to one minute, and then at lunch time I would see her by the corner store across from the school parking lot staggering, stoned out of her mind! She was stumbling, and slurring her speech trying to bum money off her fellow students to buy more downers (reds) or something to drink. Man was that awful to see since she was just so beautiful a few hours earlier and full of energy. Then just like that, she went to being doped up and begging. It was sickening to see what drugs would do and could do to a young person, So, I chose boxing and working out over the drug scene. Owning a boxing gym in the hood had its benefits; most people knew you and didn't mess with you, plus a lot of the kids (from all races) would come to the gym to workout, hang out, or just pop in and out to see who was in. It was a place you could get your frustrations out and not get into trouble.

Thirteen years old in the Chicano movement with the Brown Berets (Viva La Raza) at which time Ronald Regan was the Governor of California. At first, I enjoyed the camaraderie of the Brown Berets, then it hit me that this was not my thing and I left to play some more with my friends in Central. I didn't mind wearing the Brown Beret Khaki shirt and walking across the black bridge to the Concelio Headquarters for our meetings. What I didn't like was that most of the time, half the members didn't show up. Plus, we talked a lot of shit about the Government and did nothing to help fix the problem; our hands were tied to correct or improve the system. Then one time they gave me a gun and had me guard a guy I didn't even know what he was hiding for or who was after him. That was the end of my La Raza, Causa thing with the Berets.

Graduating from the eighth grade into high school was (as I look at it from today's view) funny. In elementary school, I was kind of popular; I can remember doing things in those years that I would never have dreamed of now, such as doing one of those talent contests in front of the school. Terry, Sammy, and I were dressed in matching pinstriped suits (Terry had white, Sammy had red, and I had green). We sang and danced to the Four Tops, Stevie Wonder, and Smoky Robinson. Damn, I was stupid back then, and then when graduation came along, we dressed in the same outfits for graduation along with the Pompadours we wore for the contest. Oh! Did I mention the white shoes, too? We were retarded, but the girls loved us and thought we were the best back then.

We kids had a lot of freedom back in the day. We would walk or bum a ride to other places outside of Central like Friday's Corner in downtown Sacramena. Friday's corner was on Fruitridge and 42nd Street; it was a community center that was a hangout for young kids on Fridays. We would drink and do drugs before we went there and dance and pick up chicks once inside. There was also the Mexican Center at Southside Park. The same old same old was happening there, too, just more Latin women to choose from, mostly from Civie Circle. The State Park had a church across the street from it that was another place to hang out during the weekend. One particular weekend, Janine and I were there partying and we forgot about the time, so I had to steal a car to get her back home before her curfew; it was a Volkswagen stationwagon. We drove around a little bit first; stopping long enough to have a little sex and makeout session. Then I dropped her off a few doors from her house since we were later than we thought. I left the vehicle down the street from my house that night and watched later the next day as the police had it towed from the neighborhood.

One neighborhood party was behind the California Elementary school in the apartment complex. I was dating Janine and I guess I had a few too many Schlitz Malt Liquors and went a little nutty. I ended up at the school busting out windows one at a time down the lower line until I hit a window with that metal safety screen in it. I cut up my hands pretty bad. So as stoned as I was, I went back to the party and Janine almost fainted looking at all the blood. She got her senses back when I explained I was all right and it wasn't so bad. She cursed me and cleaned the wounds and made everything better, if you know what I mean.

In 1968, my Dad paid cash ($37,000) for a nice home and building in the Tahoe Park neighborhood of Sacramento on 1073 Stockton Blvd. that had an attached building housing two businesses at 1075 and 1077 Stockton Blvd. One was a vacuum sales business and the other side was the vacuum repair shop. Tahoe Park was nestled between Stockton Boulevard to the west, 14th Avenue to the south, Broadway up north, and 65th Expressway just east. The gym was located on 10th Avenue and Stockton Blvd. To the west was Oak Park; at the time, it was notorious for the Black Panthers clubhouse. All that year we cleaned, painted, and installed the boxing ring, heavy bags, and all the other things needed to run and operate a boxing gym. In the end, we had a 20'x 20' (inside dimensions) ring, six heavy bags, two speed bags, two two-end bags, and an assortment of mirrors. Dad thought we should call it the California Boxing Gym since we lived in the Capital of California. At the time, there was another long-standing boxing gym in town that was above a bar called the Torch Club. The Torch Club burned down along with the gym. Julio, a long-standing top ranked boxer and family man in the Sacramena area was injured in the fire from smoke inhalation. He suffered smoke damage to his brain and was never the same. Eventually, his sons and grandsons got into the boxing arena and made a great name for themselves as well.

We moved from Central that same year when I was 13 and in the middle of my freshman year at California High School. Before I left California High, I was the Freshman Student Body Vice President. It was something I didn't campaign for; I was just nominated for the position since I was so popular (geez, imagine that). I did feel kind of funny being in a position I had no intention of staying in; I just rolled with it until we moved. J.J. was the President; Popcorn (his nickname) wasn't out of the closet as a gay dude yet, even though most people knew he was queer. He was very likable and funny in a nice way. Kind of like a girlish way, without being too gay in his actions, except when we were in the eighth grade and he got beat up by Collette; man she socked his ass up! It was funny watching him trying to fight, it was comical watching him fight like a girl, slapping and screaming while Collette was punching and talking shit in his face. Now, she should have been a boxer!

I had tried out for the football team and was kicked off the team during tryouts because of fighting. It seems I had a bad temper, so whenever I got tackled or tackled someone during practice, there would be a big dog pile and for some reason or other I would end up on the bottom. For a guy that was barely 5' 2" and weighed 100 lbs. soaking wet, that would be a lot of weight on top. Needless to say, my temper would get the best of me and I would come up swinging, usually going after the first guy I saw. Since they were all bigger than me it usually meant I had to go after them with all I had. It was all good because that meant I usually got the better of the two of us.

These temper and size things came into play when I joined the basketball team. They were all taller than me and whenever I would shoot the basketball, they would block the ball back into my face. Again, my temper got the best of me and a fight would break out, and again, I was kicked off the team. I figured then and there, that team sports were not my game.

I did try the track team; I ran cross-country and actually loved the sport. We would run wherever we felt like. Once I was running along the San Pedro beach shoreline and stepped into one of those notorious sand traps and my leg was buried down to my knee; I went down face first into the sand. I came up cracking up, with sand in my mouth and eyes, just laughing and felt so stupid. I'm just glad no one saw me.

We had a teacher, I don't remember his name (maybe I don't want to remember), but we would get him so mad at us he would have these epilepsy fits and we'd have to call the principal in to administer his medication. Another teacher we'd get mad would start yelling and his hair would come unwrapped and fall down to his collar. I can't believe he would actually wrap it around from the collar to the top of his head like a turban. He was our history teacher, I'll just call him Mr. Lincoln.

In gym class we had two gym coaches; one was Mr. Gillette, about 6'4" and over 250 lbs. The other coach's name was Mr. Schick and he stood 6' and 190 lbs. They both were fun to be around if you liked to be tortured or to hurt someone. Whenever one of us was playing our team sport for the day and committed a foul, Mr. Gillette would yell at you "take the long one…!" This meant to run once around the outside schoolyard perimeter. This meant to some of us, that if we caught up with one of the slower students we could beat them up, which is what we usually did, besides pants them. I liked Mr. Gillette; he always used my last name when he sent me off for my lap, Cheap shot Paulo…! Take the long one…! while gesturing toward the gate opening with his index finger. I can still hear and see him say it in my mind as if it was just yesterday. I tried to stay and finish my freshman year by getting a ride with my oldest brother Johnny. He was a senior and we had our first period together, which brings me to another story.

Our first period was Men's Choir. It had all different grade levels in it and we were very good singers when we weren't screwing around. One of the things that got us to screwing around was what happened before class started. Most of us got stoned on weed before class. Since my brother Johnny was a senior and drove, we would always meet at one of his friends' houses before school. It seemed if one didn't have weed, the other did. Sometimes more so than not, one of them had the stuff and we would smoke as much as we could before class. I remember, believe it or not, sometimes just going back to bed I was so stoned. There was Fernando, Tito, Van, Mitch, Bear, and Mikie, just to name a few close neighbors that would get high with us. We did do well when we sang; we actually won an award for our performance in the men's choir that year. One of the funniest moments in class was when Bro, a hardcore stud, while sitting directly in front of the piano during choir testing kept pulling out his dick and stretching it out. We were facing the piano testing our vocal cords and couldn't get away from the sight. The teacher kept having to stop we were laughing so much. As the year went on, it got harder and harder for my brother to remember to pick me up and take me home after school. So, I had to quit going to California High and enrolled in a Sacramento school called Kit Carson Junior High, which meant I got a chance to graduate again because at that time, it still had ninth grade. I got to graduate again, but I had them mail me my diploma. As for Kit Carson; it was very different for me. It had a lot of crazy black dudes in it which wasn't anything like Central and the mostly Chicano population.

I did get along with them, they were just funny crazy. I couldn't keep up with the bullshit they were dishing out at first. They were always playing the doubles or something like that, where you talk trash back and forth trying to out bullshit the other. I got pretty good at it after a while. It was definitely an experience for the new life I was about to get into. I started working for the Neighborhood Youth Center (NYC), which was the best job to ever do for a kid new to this kind of culture shock. I worked at Tahoe Elementary school as an Assistant Physical Education (PE) teacher for the kindergarten through fifth-grade students. It was good for me as a person to work and play with younger kids as well.

Luckily, I lived through the Central years of the last chapter and settled down in the south side of Sacramena in a place called Tahoe Park…

1969

I was 14 years old and stopped all the careless behaviors and started training again. Of course this didn't happen overnight. I was still getting to Central and having fun with the boys and girls. It just took a few more months than I had hoped to get into training again. The CBG opened and my boxing career started. Finally, we get the California Boxing Gym opened to the public. Right from the get-go, it was a hit! It especially was since my Dad was involved with the fight game as a professional trainer and cut man through the State Athletic Commission. So whenever they had a fight card at the Memorial Auditorium, all the out-of-town fighters came to the California Boxing Gym to train. We had some pretty big names come through there, such as George Foreman, Pepino Cueves, Bobby Chacon to name a few. Plus the local big names trained there too, such as Two-Guns, Sabe and Animal Lorenz, Squeeky Jones, Stone Cold, my brother Nathaniel, and myself. As the fight game in Sacramento grew bigger and bigger, other gyms started opening up. Eventually we were able to start concentrating on the local amateurs and that was a big hit. But again, more gyms opened up to the youth and we had more competition. We were able to prosper in the boxing field because we were community friendly and we kept our prices the same over the first 30 years we were open, $25 a month or $3 a day, until late in the 1990s when we raised the prices to $35 a month and still $3 a day. Plus with Dad paying cash for the house and gym, we didn't have a large overhead, just the basics like gas, electric, taxes, insurance, and the occasional gym equipment replacements or repairs. It was a perfect location too, right on the outskirts of Oak Park, which was a low-income neighborhood. So we had a lot of boxing clients from around Sacramena and surrounding areas.

CHAPTER 3

1970-1976 (15-21 YEARS OLD)

INTRODUCTION

The family moved from Central to Sacramena, CA and opened up the California Boxing Gymnasium. I started training again and just partying a little on the side. I moved out at 16 years old and bought my first house at 18. By the time I turned 21, I held two amateur California State Golden Glove Championships. Professionally, I held a California State title and a North American Boxing Federation (NABF) title. I was also ranked #3 by the World Boxing Council (WBC) and #6 by the World Boxing Association (WBA). I was engaged to my first love and settling down.

1970

During the first few years the gym was open, I just liked to go in there and beat the bags and exercise. It was in 1970 that a quiet guy named Richard (Richie) Kalob decided to come in and train. Richie was a lean, hard hitting mother fucker with a heart of gold (but don't let that get out). And to add to his arsenal, he had strength, endurance, and the best defense I had ever seen. Richie would come to the gym and work out by himself. Richie didn't just come in and work out, he came in and beat the bag, the speed bag, and everything he touched was beat for hours at a time. I liked watching him practice his defense, he would have these guys big and small throwing punches at him for 10 to 20 rounds, rotating them to keep fresh meat coming in. After a few months of coming in, he decided he wanted to train me. So, Richie asked my dad if it was alright if he worked with me, my dad said you better ask him yourself, so he asked and I said yes. That was just the beginning of a wonderful boxing career that goes a little like this:

The first thing Richie had me do was put my boxing gear on and try to hit him. Well you know me, free punches at somebody who wasn't going to hit back! I was all over Richie and couldn't touch him. He was just laughing, moving, and talking shit the whole time. We went a few rounds like that until he stopped me and said that's what you will learn first, defense! Because if they can't hit you, they can't hurt you! The next thing was isometric and isokinetic exercises, because if they do hit you they can't hurt you! We would train at least 2-3 hours a day, going 20 or 30 rounds with people in the gym and off the streets throwing punches at me. After a few months of that, I was pretty good at defense and eventually counterpunching too! Richie would crack me up! He would drink hard liquor at night and in the morning we would go running and I tell you! This guy could run too! He would be ahead of me smelling like whiskey and I would be behind him getting a buzz off the fumes! Finally, I had to tell him to either run the opposite way or stay the hell away from me, because I was getting lit running behind him. He told me to run faster, and to not let an old man out run me.

1971

After a full year of training with Richie and beating amateurs and professionals in the gym, we were ready for the 1971 San Francisco Examiner Golden Gloves. It was nice back then because the *San Francisco Examiner* newspaper sponsored the whole event. Since I never had any sanctioned fights under my belt, I had to put on a sparring match with some amateurs and professionals in the gym in front of the State Athletic Commission; they were in charge of the amateur boxers at the time. Since I was going into the open division of the Golden Gloves, which was for fighters with a lot of fights and no age difference, I had to show I was ready for the competition. After a few rounds with each amateur and professional, they unanimously voted to let me enter the open division of the Golden Gloves with no fights and a lot of gym experience. Needless to say, I didn't let them down. My first fight was a sensation; they put me in with the guy who was supposed to win it all, and I beat him soundly for three rounds. It was very fun for me. I was like a robot; I just kept coming in slipping, countering, bobbing, and countering some more. I was stronger and meaner than he ever imagined. The crowd loved my style and made sure I knew it, too! The second bout a few days later was a lot of the same as the first bout, except I stopped this guy in the third round to win the 1971 Bantamweight Golden Glove Championship Title, plus the trophy for fighter of the night. So, here I was just 16 years old, with two bouts under my belt in Las Vegas, Nevada representing California in the National Golden Gloves Championships. What an experience! First of all, we all received a Golden Glove Ring, a Gold Medal, nice warm-up uniforms from the *San Francisco Examiner*, and I won a trophy for fighter of the night in the finals. When the whole team got to Las Vegas (old Vegas now) we all received an 1871 silver dollar from the casino we were fighting out of (I don't remember the name) and were greeted by Archie Moore, a former World Heavy Weight Champion. Somehow my gear got lost at the airport and our sponsor bought me all new gear in time for my first bout. Let me tell you, I was in boxing heaven! They had five boxing rings going on all at once for two days, then it turned to three rings, then by the finals there was one. There was a lot of publicity from around the world, especially around a fighter name Johnny Cage; he was an ex-con who had a similar puncher style as Smokin' Joe Frasier, except he was a lightweight. Johnny looked good in his first bout; his second bout was with a tall dude who knew how to box and did just that! He boxed poor little Johnny's head off and eventually won the fight, sending Johnny home after two bouts. Ok! Back to my story. My first bout was like my first bout in San Francisco. They put me in with a guy named Renault. This Renault was supposed to win it all. He had 80 or 90 fights under his belt and was in his early 20s. Well, it only lasted two rounds; Renault had the misfortune of getting hit by one of my patented body shots and was starting to slide down the ropes. I went from his body to the head and his eyeball ran along the rope and tore open. They stopped the bout and I was declared the winner. Renault's boxing career was over, too. Now the team was down to just me in the finals and most of them went back home, except for the team coaches and a couple of other boxers who wanted to stay and savor the Nationals as much as possible. My next and last bout was in the finals against a Navy guy in his late 20s with over 100 bouts! I beat him for most of the first two rounds, but toward the end of the second round I was warned by the referee to not bob and weave. By the third round I was warned again and eventually a point was taken. I lost the bout by that one point. You got to realize back in those days, they weren't used to seeing a defensive fighter, they were used to seeing guys just beat each other up, more stand up and fight, not box. Another thing was, the guy was from the Navy, and the armed forces do not like to have their guys strictly fight for them and not be able to represent the Nation in fights with other countries. I fought one more amateur bout (and won) before the next Golden Gloves bouts in 1972.

1972

Fighting for the California State San Francisco Golden Glove Championships

It was a year later and I was feeling meaner, stronger. I had moved up a weight division into the featherweight class of 126 pounders. I even moved in with Richie and his family, wife May and son Evan. The Golden Gloves were like those the year before; I went in like gangbusters beating all three opponents down and not getting a scratch. Again, I won a trophy for bout of the night in the finals. The Nationals were in Boston this time and an old friend of boxing Tank Runnar (he was a commentator for the Big Time Wrestling show on Channel 40) invited a friend and me to the wrestling matches at the Memorial Auditorium. I took my big brother Johnny with me; we had front-row seats next to Tank and the State Athletic Commission. That's when I found out wrestling really was staged. One of the wrestlers, Jay Stevens, was on top of another wrestler named Red Basterd, and Jay was beating this guy right at our feet, when all of the sudden Red turned his head to face me and winked an eye as if to say, hey waz up? And here I was looking at him like what the fuck! After that, my whole perspective on the Big Time Wrestling was changed. Ok, back to what Tank did for me. Little did I know Tank had planned for the Athletic Commissioner to be out of the arena so he could announce my trip to Boston to represent Sacramento in the National Golden Glove

Championships! After a big standing ovation from the crowd, Tank wanted them to show their support and donate some change for the trip. He actually passed around hats and whatever he could to collect change for my trip. The collection was great; I ended up with over $250 to spend whatever way I wanted when I got to Boston. I was overwhelmed by Tank's surprise and the fans' generosity.

The flight to Boston was very memorable.

We flew in a jumbo jet that had two floors and was wide bodied. We flew over the Grand Canyon, Niagara Falls, past the Statue of Liberty, eventually landing in Boston, Massachusetts. I thought Sacramena was a big city; never again! Boston's buildings were tall! And everywhere! It was a very busy city both day and night. In the day you could hear cars, buses, trains, and horns all day! At night were the same noises plus gunfire! The hotel we stayed in was full of boxers, coaches, trainers, officials, and fans.

During my first bout, I came out swinging as usual, and beat the guy all to hell and back! I won that one pretty easily. The last bout (I only had two) was in the finals and it was almost like the final fight in last year's National Final. I was winning until they decided to take a point away for bobbing under his hooks. I ended up losing to the Air Force this time.

I had one more amateur bout; this one was at the Sacramena Memorial Auditorium. It's a nice feeling fighting in front of your friends and family in your hometown. This was back when amateurs and professionals could box on the same card. Well, I was a hit! I came out attacking to the body and head. Much stronger and meaner than this poor fool, I just kept on him for three rounds. He finally couldn't handle it any more and turned his back to me, I kept punching him on his sides, back, head, wherever I felt like until the referee dragged me off his sorry ass hanging over the second rope all out of it. The crowd went crazy! That's how you win the crowd and end your amateur career before going professional! Which I'll cover after mentioning my favorite summer of all time!

Let me back up a few years to the early summer of 1971 and Lizzie.

Ahh, the early summer of 1971, I was 16 and she was 26. We forged a bond due to a classic vehicle I owned and her need to get to work and me getting laid. It was a reckless thing to do when I think of all that could have happened if the wrong person found out, specifically her man friend. I had a 1955 Volkswagen Beetle with a ragtop, custom wheels, and a groovy 8-track tape player. Man did I have it made back then. It got even better when my best friend's (Cesar) cousin Lizzie needed a ride to work and invited me to stay for the summer. Lizzie lived in downtown Sacramena. You see, there were five of us who worked in Davis, California on a scientific ranch separating tomatoes by color off a conveyor belt. The company tested the tomatoes for something or another. All I know is we had fun, before, during, and after work. The mornings started with me kicking Lizzie out of the bed to cook breakfast, and then having her sneak back into bed for a little early morning booty call. I was always a morning person and didn't mind the wakeup call or being the designated driver, especially since I was the only one who had a car. Lizzie and I would then go to Central and pick up my best friend Cesar, then the Canto sisters (Amy and Faye). All of us were the same age but were growing at different paces. Faye had big boobs already, and her sister Amy had a body like a 2x4, straight and narrow. They were all afternoon people which made the initial drive to Davis a little boring except for the fact that in my mind I knew something they didn't; I was laying a 26-year-old woman. During the day while we worked, Lizzie and I would joke around and grab each other's business, (if you know what I mean) and laugh. It was such a turn-on; all day we would tease each other. Sometimes Cesar and I would tease the Canto sisters, too. After all, they were nice looking, too, and we didn't want to seem rude. After work, I would drive everyone home tired yet feeling good about ourselves since we did get along really well. When the evening came after a shower or during, so would Lizzie. I tell you, she was like a sex maniac, always on the prowl for some thrills and excitement. Sometimes her man friend Poncho would show up. Let me explain Poncho to you; he was about 36, muscular, rode in on a Harley, partied with Hells Angels, was a former Green Beret, and could be as mean as a junkyard dog, fleas and all. He would drink beer with an Old Granddad #7 chaser, smoke weed with Lizzie and sometimes take her to the bedroom and make her squeal like a banshee. Yet, when he was done (and he was usually done pretty quickly), Lizzie would take a shower and let me know that it was nothing by giving me a blowjob. She was so weird like that; I didn't really think anything of their relationship except that he was using her as a pit stop between riding and partying. I think he was supporting her as well so she felt obligated to do something for him, which meant a little boom boom and food before his next adventure.

Eventually, I told Cesar about his cousin and me. He told me she had already told him. We started cracking up and you know how 16-year-old guys are, he asked the questions and I gave the answers. Cesar was a little worried about Poncho finding out and made sure Lizzie and I kept things behind closed doors, which we did. The next thing you know at work the touching and feeling got a little more risky. After work got to be more fun too. Lizzie and I would be at a hamburger joint and she would see me looking at another women and start telling me off (playfully) saying, "you bastard, how could you look at another woman when we're going to have a baby! You don't love me anymore do you? I'm getting fat and you won't touch me, you son-of-a-bitch! Go get her if that's what you want!" Me, I would just look at her like she was crazy, and the other unknowing poor girl would look at me like I was a no-good so-and-so. I would just shake my head and laugh. Lizzie could be such a crack-up. Some of our sexcapades included a time we were hiking with a group of attorney friends she had. We'd sneak off the trail and smoke a joint and get naked (well, half naked), and I sat on a rock with her on top and we did the boom boom in the forest. Man, did I feel like yelling like Tarzan after that. When we met up with the rest of the crowd they were all looking at us kind of like we were caught doing something guilty. Then there was the time we were on the rocks at Negro Bar in Folsom. It was early morning around 10:30. I was on a fold–out recliner/chair and she moved her bikini bottom over just enough for penetration on the beach. Talk about an exhibitionist! Luckily, we were away from the main crowd and partially hidden by some rocks. I tell ya, she was some kind of woman. The only bad thing about the whole mess was we actually started to like each other. But because of her predicament with Poncho, I was not going to rock the boat. I wanted to live to see 17. Besides it never would have worked out anyway; she was actually over sexed for me. By the end of the summer I moved into my own place and never looked back. As for Lizzie, she ended up pregnant by some other dude and had a beautiful little girl. She stopped living the way she was and settled down and married a man 25 years her senior. They still live together and her daughter is very bright, married, and has a child of her own. When you ask, what was the best summer I ever had? I will always say with a smile, the summer of '71. It didn't end there either! I met Victoria right after leaving Lizzie in the late summer of '71.

My first love, late summer of 1971.

Victoria was her name. She was ½ Filipina on her dad's side (Reyes), and ¼ American Indian and ¼ Spanish on her mom's side (Stella), and at 15½ was the most beautiful woman I had ever seen! We meet through Chita (Chita was mentioned in the last chapter), he actually dated Victoria a couple of times before I saw her at the Mexican Center across from South Side Park. The Mexican Center was where us young teens would go to dance and just meet other people our age. I remembered her right off the bat! She was beautiful, with her raven black hair, hazel eyes, and the exotic Asian look she had with the gorgeous body. We hung around there for a little while and left in my 1969 Camaro Rally Sport (it was a clean vehicle). I can still taste our first kiss; it was gentle yet passionate. Victoria had a nice taste to her; I can never get her out of my mind. On our next date, we went to the Japanese Bazaar on Riverside and Broadway. We danced to a Japanese band that played Tower of Power music all night. Before the night was over, our song was "Sparkling in the Sand" (at least in my mind it was!). After a few more drinks and dancing, we took off to Discovery Park down by the fork of the Sacramento and American Rivers. The night was warm, clear, and had a full moon to make our first encounter very romantic, especially since it was on the beach at the American River side. Victoria's body was the most beautiful body I had ever seen, I was in love for the first time in my young life! After that we were inseparable, except for the fact that I lived on the other side of town and she lived in Old Central. Every chance I had, I was over at her house talking to her. She was going through a breakup with this other guy at the time and once it was finalized, we got a lot closer. Victoria's father was a short handsome man with a quiet strength about him. I liked helping him around the house when he let me. As for Stella, she wasn't too thrilled about me, we sort of bumped heads a few times, probably my fault, since I was over there all the time and a little cocky, too! At the time, I was getting back into the boxing. Actually, I was getting ready to fight in the Golden Gloves of 1972 (from

34

the boxing chapter). It was kind of funny, we had the one Boom Boom, and then it took another year until she got on the pill and let me have it again. After that, it was on all the time!

1972

I can remember the phone call from Victoria saying she was on the pill and that we could start having sex (well, she didn't say it exactly like that! But, that's what I heard!). We made plans for that evening (I don't remember what they were) that didn't happen! I do remember picking her up from her house and going straight to my place and just going Neanderthal man on her. She started cracking up and told me she knew I would do that. You gotta understand the many times we would be in front of her house making out and me leaving with blue balls from grinding and kissing all the time. She had a way of making me so hot! For both of us being so young, we knew a lot about each other's body and when and where to touch. We were spiritually connected, mind, body, soul, and heart. I miss the way we could just talk about anything and the way we made each other laugh all the time! I really love and miss our special times and connection we had. It wasn't long before she graduated from high school and we moved in together into an apartment off 27th and V Streets. At first it was fine, and then I started getting into the celebrity status in my boxing and was out all the time without her. She was still working on her education and working part-time while I was working across the street at the Farmers' Market on 28th and Broadway and fighting professionally.

1973

We finally made it through the tough times and decided to buy a house in Del Paso Heights; it was a nice Brick house, sitting on a corner lot, with two bedrooms and a den, two ponds, and three fireplaces. We bought it off a couple of former Marines for $22,000.00. One fireplace was in the living room, another was in the den, and the third was in the backyard. That was the best one because it had a barbeque pit built to one side of it with horseshoe-shaped seating to complete it. One of the ponds was built close by to make the BBQ more relaxing.

1976

I'm going to finish talking about my relationship with Victoria before I get back to 1971. As my boxing career started to end and I was eventually stripped of my boxing license (see the professional boxing career later in this chapter), I joined the Marines. It was one of those things I always wanted to be (a Sergeant in my Marine Corps!) since I was a young kid growing up in Central. The bad thing about it was, I didn't even talk about it with Victoria; I just joined with my friend Rudy in the Buddy System on November 19, 1976.

During my time in Boot Camp I felt Victoria and I were getting closer; little did I know she was drifting away from me. Graduation from Boot Camp was very memorable for me. It was the first time I had seen her in three months and she looked absolutely beautiful. She had a wonderful glow to her and her gentle, silent touch made me feel like my life couldn't get better. When we got into Sacramena, we registered into a motel off 16th Street, which to this day I get all fuzzy inside when I pass it. I sometimes wonder why she started crying for some unknown reason after making love that first night from Boot Camp. My first duty station was on top of the hill at Camp Margarita Ville (Camp Margarita home of the Second Battalion, Fifth Marines was the real name). Soon we were engaged to be married (that didn't last long). I would come home on leave every chance I could and after a while, every time I left, I felt I was leaving Victoria for good; it was an awful feeling. The one I remember the most was when we were at the Greyhound bus terminal on 11th and I Streets. As the bus pulled out, I could see my beautiful Victoria with tears in her eyes standing on a corner block of the terminal and watching my bus pull away. She looked so sad, it made me tear up. Still when I pass the old terminal, I can imagine her standing there and the look on her face as I rode away. Less than a week later and a week before we were to get married, Victoria called to let me know we were through, we were not going to get married and she did not want to see me again. I had never felt this kind of pain before and didn't really know how to handle it! This breakup came as a surprise to me and was like a cheap shot in the dark. All I can remember is feeling lost and walking into my Platoon Commander's office and telling him what had happened. I also told him I had to go home and kick her out of my house, talk to her, and a whole lot of other things that came to my mind. I really had mixed feelings about what was happening. I wanted to cry, hurt her, hurt myself; I really wasn't thinking too clearly. Either way, I was given three days to get my affairs in order and to stay out of trouble. I packed up the bike and was going over 130 miles per hour on the freeway when I was pulled over by a CHP officer. He was trembling and ready to beat my ass when I told him why I was going so fast. For some unknown reason, he felt my pain and let me go with just an 80 mile per hour ticket and a warning that if I so much as went over the speed limit by one mile per hour while in his jurisdiction, he would haul my ass in and beat me, too! The officer actually followed me out of his jurisdiction and when I was safely out, he waved me on. By the time I got to Sacramento and off the freeway at Richards Blvd. on that very cold evening, my whole body was frozen. I tried to put my foot down at the stop light on Richards Blvd. and my leg was frozen and I couldn't straighten it out and almost dropped the bike on myself. After cursing Victoria and the cold, I was able to keep the bike from dropping. Sometimes I can still feel the cold on my legs when I get off the freeway at Richards Boulevard. I was able to see Victoria at her sister's apartment the next day. We talked for a little while, and then I had to ask if she was seeing someone else; she said yes. I was hurt worse than any boxing match or street fight I was ever in. It got worse when I had to ask if she had slept with him and she said yes. My emotions took over and I slapped her face knocking her out of her chair! I couldn't believe what I had done or, for that matter, what she had told me. I wanted to jump through the second story window and just die (I would never be the same after this moment).

1976 Aug. 22 Sacramena, CA: 1. Disorderly conduct: Loiter/refuse ID 2. Obstructs/resists public officer.

Received Dear John letter from fiancé while in the Marine Corps in San Diego took military leave to address the issue. Her sister called police when I went to her house to talk to her, apparently thinking I was there to beat up my ex-fiancé's new boyfriend (I did not know he was there) once the police got there it did not go too well.

1976 Sept. 01 Sacramena, CA: 1. Disorderly conduct: Loiter/refuse ID.

I tried to talk to my ex-fiancé again and was arrested. When I went back to my duty station, I eventually put in for overseas duty and remained there until my Honorable Discharge as a Weapons Company, Weapons Platoon Sergeant.

I went back to Camp. We tried to talk (I tried) and make things right, but it was not to be. I volunteered to go overseas and was granted the opportunity within days. I went on a fucking spree; I hated women, especially overseas, since I was surrounded by Asian women that reminded me of Victoria. I hurt all the time and actually had a death wish. I didn't care what happened to me and I guess that made me a better Marine. It wasn't long before I made Sergeant in my beloved Marine Corps. In doing so, I was offered a lot of positions, such as Officer's Candidate School, Paratroopers school, Sniper school, and Platoon Sergeant. I turned some of them down and the others were given to Marines with more time in the Corps than me (I'll tell you about that when I get to the Marine Corps Chapter). Victoria and I kept in touch off and on (one or two times per year) for over 30 years until 2005 when she started to feel guilty about sneaking behind her husband's back, as she called it, and told me she couldn't talk to me anymore. I really wanted and enjoyed our talks. I would kind of keep her up on my life and she would do the same. We were friends who had a lot in common and a past that nobody could take away. Eventually, that too was taken from me. It's like they say and what you hear in songs about never forgetting your first love and all that surrounded those moments in time. I can hear those songs and still feel the love I lost so long ago and feel the pain that came with it. I have to admit, it was my fault and I will take the blame for my stupidity and how I acted, resulting in Victoria's actions. Knowing this, I will always thrive to be a better person for all those I bring into my life.

Let's back up a few years. In 1971, my first purchased vehicle was a 1955 Volkswagen Ragtop bug. It was light blue with large Kragen rims in back and smaller ones in the front, with an 8-track tape player, an egg-shaped rear window, a donut steering wheel, and a left and right blinker system arm that came out of the side like an arm that lit up; it was very unique. The Ragtop went all the way to the back of the rear window so you got plenty of sunshine and wind. It even had a gas switch on the floorboard because it didn't have a gas gauge. So you had to keep an eye on the odometer and when you did run out of gas all you had to do was kick the switch over and it went right into the reserve tank. But the most unique thing about this bug was the bottom pan that covered the whole bottom of the vehicle. Because of this pan you could drive it in water and float; as long as you kept it running at a high revolution it would actually float like a boat. I actually tried it at Folsom lake when the lake was over-filled and the parking lot was full of water. I drove it out a few hundred feet and back, just to test it.

I bought my first motorcycle from Tino; it was a Honda 160 bored to a 205. I ran the shit out of that bike! My final ride was by the river where we would party. There were motocross bike trails there that were tested at times and, well, on this one trail, there were two hills about 30 feet high with a dip that was about 20 feet wide in the middle. I didn't quite make the speed needed to clear the dip and landed smack dap in the middle, busting my balls and the bike's back rim. I laid there for a good half hour gently rubbing my balls, moaning and groaning until I had enough strength to get up and ride the bike out of there. The bike's back rim was bent all to shit and was wobbling all the way home. My balls didn't like that ride, but I had no choice. I could barely stand, let alone push a bike. I ended up selling the bike to Georgian for a $100 dollars and within a few days Georgian had the rims straightened out and was riding around.

1972

I was working at Campbell's Soup and had enough money in my pockets to buy a 1969 Camaro Rally Sport. I bought it from my cousin Boy on my mom's side. It was only a few years old and had a nice cassette stereo system, and was clean and fast with its 350 motor. Boy, and I never exchanged the pink slip; I just took over payments and paid him. The only problem was that he never paid the bank and the vehicle was repossessed within one year. I wanted to kick his ass but my dad talked me out of it.

1973

My next vehicle was a Galaxy 500. It was a nice darker blue with custom rims and tires and a shiny black vinyl top. The interior was very clean and the 8-track tunes were groovy! It had four doors too, my first four-door vehicle. At about the same time, I purchased a 750 Honda motorcycle and started to fix it up before I went into the Marine Corps. I left it with my brother Johnny while I was in the Corps and he wrecked it a few times and put it back together even better than before. The bike looked like a Harley with the duel oversized tank and duel exhaust, pull-back handlebars and highway pegs, extended front forks with the frame cut and leveled, and the paintjob was a custom blue too. The bike sat low and long like a street pro Harley. I got a lot of compliments on the bike wherever I rode. When I got out of the Corps, I drove it to a local car dealership and traded it straight across for a nice Cougar. The bike was so clean they had me leave it on their showroom floor!

I've already told you about some of the schools I went to but not about American Legion Adult High. The reason I ended up at American Legion was because I was working at Campbell's Soup at night and not putting enough hours in at Johnson High. The counselor at Johnson told me my grades were staying up, it was just that I needed to put the time in for justification to the school district. They suggested American Legion and so goes the story. American Legion was an adult school for mostly screw-ups, pregnant girls, funny guys, troublemakers, and stoners. About 90% of the women there were pregnant or had kids and were pregnant. The school had what I liked, a motor vehicle shop class and a cooking class. The shop class was nice because we could bring our own vehicles in and work on them for credits. A couple of the guys had nice vehicles, but others had pieces of shit. The cooking class was a co-ed class that was also a sex education class every other day. The school was mostly closed in with dark hallways and hardly any ventilation. So just before the guys' cooking class, you could smell the weed smoked in the hallways. We guys could cook up a storm after a few puff puffs! We would share our food with the girls in the sex education class because they would do the same when they cooked. The sex education class was funny and a little too late for the girls in there, since most of them were already pregnant. I liked the students in the school because of their attitudes. They were funny and real; we never really argued, mostly talked a lot of shit and got along, not like at Johnson High; it might have been the smoke we shared. When it came to the graduation ceremony, I had them send me my diploma since I had worked late the night before at Campbell's Soup.

My first job in Sacramena was at Tahoe Park Elementary School through the Neighborhood Youth Center (NYC) as an Assistant Physical Education Instructor. I liked working with the kids and they liked me, especially the little girls; a few of them had crushes on me and would beat some of the boys up if they didn't listen to me.

My second job was with Campbell's Soup working night shifts on the high-second floor cleaning out the large two-story aluminum vats that held the hot soup. We had to work in twos because of the time table affiliated with the vats. We had a certain amount of time to climb in, clean, and rinse the vats before the hot soup was funneled in for processing. One time, Ralphie and I were stoned and fell asleep in there and all of the sudden we hear somebody beating on the outside vat and yelling that the soup was coming! We grabbed our cleaning tools and climbed out of there without even rinsing the vat. We made it out by seconds. We also had fun times in the vats; we would hold the aluminum tops like shields and have the water hoses in the other hand and shoot at each other and anyone else that came by. On our breaks we would grab a bag full of fresh cooked meats that would be processed for the soups and a few vegetables and go to the high-second floor roof to watch the movies at the drive-in across the street. I must have watched Raquel Welch in *One Million Years BC and Kansas City Bomber*, a Roller Derby movie, a dozen times. I also saw the *Planet of the Apes* movies up there. Ralphie and I would get loaded and eat our snacks and watch the movies from the comfort of the roof. The reason I liked hanging with Ralphie so much was because he was fat and funny and his dad was our supervisor and he let us get away with doing what we did most of the time. One time, I was so stoned I locked myself in my locker and fell asleep propped up in there. Luckily, the locker has a mechanism in there that allowed me to get out from inside it. I worked out of the Teamsters Union Hall for a few years after that as a Lumper, loading and unloading trucks at grocery and freight warehouses. That kept me in shape and busy; it's what my dad did most of his life in Sacramena until he retired.

My next job was at a Farmers' Market owned by the Kong family. The Kong family had a nice chain of grocery stores in and around the

Sacramento area in the 1950s through the 1970s. Most of the employees were Chinese and a part of their family. At our store on 28th and Broadway, there were only four of us who were not Kong family. There was an American Indian as the butcher, Shirley, an older white lady, was a cashier and accountant, and Jack was a young white kid with long blondish hair who worked as a cashier and stocker. I worked as a bag boy and stocker. The work was easy and fun most of the time. The customers were mostly minorities from the surrounding neighborhoods such as Oak Park and Downtown Sacramena. Back then, California still had welfare stamps programs for the people in need. So, on the 1st and the 15th of the month we would be very busy dealing with the crazy ghetto people. Some of them were just plain nasty, leaving their dirty diapers full of shit in the shelves or eating food while shopping and leaving the half-eaten goods on the floor or shelf. Some would actually just bring the empty bag or wrapper to the cashier and pay for it, others would not. I lived across the street and a few blocks down from the store with Victoria as told in Victoria's story. That was a nice convenience. I was also boxing professionally at the time. It helped the store with publicity and the customers liked to be on TV as I was being filmed for my next fight. Amos was my dad's partner when he opened the California Boxing Gym. Amos was the meanest old man I ever met. He cursed all the time and didn't have anything good to say about anybody. Believe it or not, he even tried to run for the Mayor of Sacramena. I don't think he had a clue because of all the cursing he did, he didn't have a chance of winning the job. When I was barely 16 years old, Amos got sick and needed someone to stay with his wife and him on 50th and T Streets. I would help Amos get in and out of bed when he needed me. I also helped his wife Mini try and keep him in check. He was very mean to her and would always curse and act up. I remember coming home one evening from a night of partying and he knew it. So, after around an hour of sleeping he starts hollering at me to get up and help him go to the can. What an asshole! Poor little Mini, she kept telling him that I just got home and that she could help him but no! He wanted to teach me a lesson and get my ass up tired or not! Amos got sick later that month and was sent to the hospital. During his stay Mini got ill and died. We didn't want to tell Amos until he got a little better. Once we told him that Mini had passed he gave up and died two days later.

I moved back home for a few months before Rich wanted me to move in with him, May, and their son Evan. I liked it there in the Greenhaven area of South Sacramena. May was the typical wife in that she went to work and came home and cooked and cleaned for us. She was very beautiful and had a nice round booty that was a sight to see. I also liked to hear her sing around the house as she went about her business. She did have a temper though. One day, Rich was a little liquored up and he made the mistake of pissing her off. She got the gun and chased him out of the house for a few hours. I picked him up and we went for a ride and just bullshitted until he was able to call her up and smooth things over enough to go home without her wanting to shoot him.

1973-1975

Back to me beating other fighters up!

Before I get started on my career in boxing, I feel I need to tell you about Sacramena and its boxing history. Sacramena had its fair share of world-class boxers back in the '60s, '70s, '80s, '90s, and into the year 2000. We had the Savala's from their Father Trino to Richard and Mario and other Savalas. There were the Lopez brothers Sal and Tony "The Tiger," Stan Ward, Timmy Miller, my brother Nathanial, Loreto Garza, Tino Huggins, Richard "Boom Boom" Duran, The Brooks brothers Tim and Mark, Bobby Chacon came late in his career, and Diego Corrales came later in the '90s and 2000. Bobby, Diego, and Tony the Tiger were the most famous of us all. They had the fighting style most boxing fans liked to watch. They were relentless and basically beat their opponents down and had chins like penitentiary steel. Back in the day it wasn't unusual to see big posters on walls and at barber shops and restaurants with the latest fight card. The main place to watch a fight in Sacramena was the Memorial Auditorium. It was small but nice enough for everybody to see the action. Later the main place to go was Arco Arena; it was very large but didn't quit have the ambiance of the Memorial Auditorium.

As a Professional Fighter, I was a very mean, lean, fighting machine. I had the strength, conditioning, and defense to take on all comers. My first three bouts were easy wins, going six rounds instead of the conventional four rounds. By my fourth bout I was going eight rounds and starting to feel much better at attacking the body. My knockouts were coming by way of a vicious body attack. It was much easier on my hands, too! My first 10 rounds were with a Black Dude named Freddie Golan. Freddie was built short and very muscular, plus was in excellent shape. I had never been hit so hard in all my life; Freddie hit me with a left hook to the temple that had me seeing black for a second. After that hit, I knew I was in trouble, so I started digging to his body like my life depended on it, and it did! After the sixth round, the body shots were starting to take their toll on Freddie. His body movement was slower and he wasn't hitting with as much authority as in the first few rounds. I ended up taking a unanimous decision in a fight that I will always remember.

After 11 fights, I was ready for the world ranked professionals. On my 12th bout, I took on Eddie Duran for the vacant California State Bantamweight title. Eddie came in with a record of 16–0–0 with 14 knockouts. He left with a good ass whipping and no title. I have to tell you, it was a very hard-fought battle. Eddie was known for his hard punching; that's when I found out punchers cannot fight moving backwards. Because that's what I did; I just kept beating on him, and using my defense and strength to keep the momentum on my side, relentlessly beating him down and pushing forward. He never gave up; he just hung in there with me until the final bell.

My next bout was for the Vacant North American Boxing Federation Title as a Bantamweight against a Puerto Rican from New York named Vito Vallez. The bout was in Sacramena at the Memorial Auditorium in front of a sellout crowd. I didn't fail my hometown crowd. Vito was a short fighter, about 5' 2" who had good boxing skills but no strength. I did my basic thing and took it to him, beating him up pretty good to win the North American Boxing Federation Title, which got me rated in the top 10 in the world. I was officially rated #3 by the World Boxing Council (WBC) and #6 by the World Boxing Association, (WBA), not bad for only having 13 bouts!

My next bout was one of those opportunities that don't come around very often in the fight business. I was offered a shot at one of the world titles if I got past a fighter named Juanito Vayes. Juanito was undefeated in 32 bouts with 31 of them coming by way of knockout. The winner of our bout would be fighting Alonzo Zapata who was the main event on our boxing card fighting against Soon Wan Kong for the vacant WBC Bantamweight title. Alonzo was undefeated with a record of 20 wins, all by knockout. The bout was for a new promoter I had never used before. I usually had Kid Tanner and Babes Burch, and this time around it was Max Raider and his wife Irene. Max was a big time promoter out of Los Angeles. The fight was held in Inglewood, California at the Forum Auditorium. I can remember thinking when I first met Juanito Vayes at the weigh-ins; I looked at him and thought to myself how skinny and ruff (ugly) looking he was. He didn't look like all the hype that followed him. He didn't speak English but he was polite. I respected that in a fighter. Most people thought I shouldn't have taken the fight, that I wasn't ready for such a big step in the fight world. I knew I was ready physically, mentally, and experience wise. Plus, I didn't want to fight 30 or 40 fights before I got a chance at a World Title. So, I went to the Forum with Salsa (my corner man and Rich Kalob's second training coordinator) and Lucca Gambino (my cut man). Walking into the ring was an experience! The Forum was sold out! No one but Mexicans were there to watch their favorites beat up on us so-called Mexican-Americans. I noticed a few of my friends from Central there (Big George, Dennis, and a few others. I can't remember all their names right now). Those crazy Mexicans were throwing their beers at me and acting like they wanted to attack me. Luckily, security knew what to do and that was to keep moving toward the ring and don't stop. After being rushed into the ring and all the announcements, we got to fight. As usual, I got busy beating on Juanito's body and head. I felt much stronger than him yet a little awkward since he was the same height as me, usually I fought shorter fighters. I was doing good and felt I was winning the fight on sheer strength and defense. In the third round, all of a sudden I got hit square on the top of my lip and right below my nose, the punch made my gums swell so much that my top front teeth pulled back towards my throat. This made it impossible to close my mouth or clinch my teeth. It didn't hurt but I couldn't close my mouth and so I decided between rounds as I was sitting on the stool that I would go out and try and finish him off in the next round. I told Salsa and Lucca the problem and they agreed that it was better to try and stop him and if not, at least I would not end up with a broken jaw or get knocked out. So, I went out there and treated that round like a street fight! I attacked and just kept on him never backing off. Juanito took some good punches and fought back and never seemed too worried or out of control; he was definitely a great fighter. After that round, when the referee came to our corner we called the fight. I was very disappointed, mainly because the fight was stopped because of a $1 mouthpiece we used. I had used it in all those other fights and it worked for me, this time I should have had a professional one made. It was a hard lesson to learn.

My next two fights were almost carbon copies of each other, explained as follows. My first fight was with Bobby "Hands" Rubalcava 14-2-0 out of Renosa, Mexico. Everyone knew that if you fought in Mexico you would have to beat or knockout the Mexican if you were to win. The California State Athletic Commission advised us that they would be there to make sure the fight was fair. So, my intentions were to just beat the hell out of this guy and leave no doubt as to who won. After we got there, we had to wait another week before we could fight because of a hurricane 100 miles from shore. That was why the Commission could not be there and view the fight for fairness. Even though I beat this guy for 12 rounds and cut and bruised him up pretty good, I still lost the decision. I didn't feel too bad though because most of the hometown crowd came to my dressing room to congratulate me on the fight. Even José Napoles, the reigning World Welterweight Champion, came to my dressing room and said I looked great and had won the fight!

Then I went to San Juan, Puerto Rico to fight Fredo Gonzalez 6-0-1. San Juan was a beautiful Island and the women! Oh, my gosh! They were from dark-skinned, nappy-haired, big boobed beauties to blonde-haired, green-eyed, big booties, light complexioned ladies. They all spoke the beautiful Puerto Rican language. I felt so much love from inside, like I belonged with these people. The San Juan Hotel was next to the ocean and had two large casinos in it and six restaurants that were for suit and tie only. They had one restaurant for casual eating. I was lucky enough to be there when they were having a cosmetology and hair dressing competition going on in the hotel. The most beautiful women in all of Puerto Rico, and the world for that matter, were in the house! OK! Back to the fight story, I was supposed to weigh 118 lbs. for the fight with Fredo. I was feeling pretty good when May (my trainers' wife) and I arrived in San Juan. Everything was arranged for us when all of the sudden there was a hurricane 100 miles off the coast of Puerto Rico and the fight got pulled back for another two days. The gym we went to was not that great and because of the few days delay I decided not to spar, just beat the bags and work up a good sweat trying to stay at 118 lbs. Then the fight was postponed another two days, and then another until it was almost two weeks before we fought. I was still trying to stay at 118 lbs. In between this were the women of Puerto Rico in the hotel all day long, in and out. It was maddening! By the time we made the fight at the Roberto Clemente Coliseum in San Juan, Puerto Rico, I was not as strong or mean as I usually was. I started out hard and fast as usual, taking it to Fredo. I could see in his eyes that he was scared of me and I tried to capitalize on it. But, after a few rounds of beating on him, I started to lose my strength and gas. I could tell he felt my loss and he started to take it to me like I had done to so many other fighters in the past and bam! He hit me with a solid shot to the solar plexus and I was down at the end of the round. I made the count to end the round. I knew I had nothing left and in between rounds I called the fight. For some reason, I didn't feel too bad, maybe because I was too weak or just not into the fight as usual. That was another loss, and another lesson learned. Earlier I wanted to cancel the fight because of the weight and delays, but May thought that because of all the money and expense to make the flight and the fight that I should just tough it out and fight anyway, my mistake. We should have renegotiated the weight and the purse, my bad.

My loss at the hands of a nobody in Stockton was the last straw! I beat this Geronimo up for all ten rounds and got head butted in the last 30 seconds of the fight. The referee stopped the bout and gave Geronimo the win. The crowd went wild and started fighting, throwing chairs, and drinks. I just walked away disappointed with boxing. I still trained and kept busy in the gym, but I just wasn't into it.

Then my brother Nathanial had a fight at the Memorial Auditorium and got knocked out by some bum. After the fight was stopped, I got in the ring and tried to help him up. As I was holding him up in his corner, the trainer from the other side came over and wanted to congratulate him. I told him not now; he was still a little out of it. That's when the trainer grabbed my shoulder and pulled me back! As I was pulled, I threw a solid left hook to this man and knocked him down. The next thing you know, there were other fights going on in the ring. I look over to my right and

TH E STORY TELLER

there was this big guy outside the ring with his arm around my dad's neck, so my brother Johnny and I grabbed this guy's arms and spread him out enough for my dad to land a solid right to his chin and knock him two rows back. Then as I was turning around, I saw a punch coming my way; I bobbed and came up with another left hook to knock this fool out. Before we knew it, the ring was jammed with spectators and security. What a lot of fun that was! As I was leading my stupid brother Nathanial out of the ring, he came to and started to yell, "who hit my dad?" I told him to shut the fuck up, and if he didn't go out partying and acting a fool we wouldn't be in this predicament.

1976

Well, we had a nice run in the boxing arena and on the home front. After having my boxing license suspended, I went and joined the Marines, one of my life long dreams was about to happen...

CHAPTER 4

1977-1983 (22-28 YEARS OLD)

INTRODUCTION

My boxing license was taken away for illegal fighting, so at 22, I joined the Marine Corps to be a Sergeant. Within a few months I experienced the most horrific event that could happen to a young military man; I received a Dear John over the phone from my fiancé I was to marry in just one week. Within 10 months and 3 weeks, I transferred overseas and was honorably promoted to a corporal (E-4). In 1978, I was ranked a sergeant (E-5) in my beloved Marine Corps; it was a very proud moment in my life. When I got out of the Marine Corps, I went on a partying rampage. Somehow, I still managed to go to school and get Solar Utilization Certified, actually building and installing Solar systems. My first job was as a Pipe Fitter on Fort Ord.

Nov 19, 1976-1979

I'm a Marine at 22. I joined the Marine Corps on the Buddy Plan with my old friend Rudy. He joined as a grunt (infantry) and I joined to be an Engineer. We went to Oakland earlier that week to the Armed Forces Entry and Exams (AFEES) building. That was where all young recruits went to get a two-day exam of all body parts (both in and outer parts). All day we were waiting in one line or another to get tested. They took more blood than I thought they should, checked so far up my ass than I thought they should, and that was where I found out I was color blind (which explained a lot about my choice of clothing growing up). After two days of testing, we ended up home for a few more days before being called to boot camp.

I remember having a nice little going away party with Victoria and a few close friends. I was really looking forward to going to boot camp and can remember Victoria not liking it too much. We did have a very nice evening after the party and did talk a lot about our future. She was very sad and I was satisfied; I was going to be a Marine!

Our first two weeks at San Diego's Marine Corps Recruit Depot (MCRD), Boot Camp, we were in receiving barracks. That was where we waited until enough new recruits joined to form a Company (250 total). It was kind of exciting at first. We caught a bus from the Sacramento Recruiter's Office, and on the way down to San Diego we picked up a few more recruits, arriving in San Diego around midnight. As we pulled into MCRD, I looked around at all the different people on the bus and tried imagining how they would do under pressure. Well, it didn't take long to find out. That was where the fun began! It was just like I imagined. As soon as we got to a stop and the doors opened on the bus (it was around midnight), two Genuine Marine Corps Drill Sergeants came hollering, cursing, spitting with every word, grabbing, pulling, and rushing us out of the bus and onto those famed yellow footprints. After another ½ hour of cursing and hollering, we were lead into a warehouse to receive our clothing and equipment. Of course nothing was sized, it was just, oh! He's a size medium or he's a size small like my sister. Then we changed and turned in our old clothing and equipment. That's where they thought I was a perverted drug addict for having all those playboy magazines and vitamins. We finally got to hit the rack by 0230 that morning. There wasn't much said that night from most of us, just a few crying because of the abuse we endured earlier. But what did they expect? That was the Marine Corps!

The next morning came real quick; 0530 they were at it again! This time they were throwing garbage cans and tipping over racks! Man I loved that stuff! As we were all standing there at a civilian position of attention, they told us how they wanted the barracks cleaned up, and as we were doing what they wanted, they were right behind us messing it up hollering that it was not the way they said to do it! So, while this was going on for another 15 minutes they were also telling us the plans for the day. In order we will shit, shave, shower, line up for chow, eat, and then get our Marine Corps issued haircut. I thought I would be funny and deny them the haircut, which I did (I came in with a bald head) but it cost me 50 pushups after being yelled at for not wanting to be uniform with the rest of my recruits. I was also told to grow it now!!! Which we both knew wasn't going to happen, but I agreed. The next few weeks got to be an adventure all its own. We studied the Marine Corps Handbook, which has all the rules and regulations according to the Uniform Code of Military Justice. We exercised and marched, marched and exercised. Then it started to happen, some of the guys were starting to break. One would stand by himself at a position of attention and just stare ahead, the other acted like he was on a motorcycle and make noises and ride around the barracks, the other cursed a Colonel out and spit on his uniform. He was taken away to the brig and from what we heard, had to spend three months in there before being sent to another Company to finish out his boot camp time. It was close to two weeks and still we had to endure the down time. So, they had their way with us. Then it was my turn; I was on the second floor of the barracks with our platoon studying when the Drill Instructor ordered me to get a pencil from the lower barracks platoon. When I arrived in the other Platoon's barracks I was to yell, Sir! Recruit Paulo requesting a pencil, Sir! Apparently, the Drill Instructor thought I was a spy and ordered me out of their barracks. I went back up to our Drill Instructor and tried to explain what had happened. He in turn, started cursing and yelling at me that I was a no good, piece of shit and that I couldn't even retrieve a lousy pencil from a bunch of pussies. He then ordered me back downstairs to get a pencil, which I proceeded to do. This time when I arrived at their doorstep, the Drill Instructor threatened to send the platoon after me if I interrupted them again. He then proceeded to run me off. I ran back upstairs stopping half-way thinking about my dilemma. When I did arrive back upstairs, luckily the Drill Instructor had found a pencil and ordered me back downstairs to apologize to the other Drill instructor for interrupting his class. That didn't go too well either; he sent his platoon after me, and they didn't catch me but did run up to my barracks where we held them off. It was all good clean fun; too bad it was at my expense!

Did I mention the exercising? Whenever we pissed off the Sergeants or

Corporals, they would have us stop, hit the deck, and proceed to do either bends and trusts, mountain climbers, push-ups, sit-ups, or leg lifts. We seemed to be doing a lot of these exercises, which was good for preparing us for the actual training we were about to endure. The marching and running were needed as well. I tell you what! They kept us busy all day! And when we ate, we ate everything. It started to get really boring. I wanted to learn how to kill, maim, and destroy the enemy, besides shoot rifles, mortars, machine guns, and other weapons of mass destruction. My whole attitude changed when I was given two minutes to hit the can and pee. As I was in there, I heard someone call out; Hey You! Asshole! (My father used to call me that all the time and after a while I thought that was my name) so when I turned around, there stood a short Latin man dressed up as a Marine Corps Sergeant calling me an asshole! As I turned around I smiled (which I shouldn't have done) almost pissing on him. He started calling me a puto and that I must have wanted to fuck him because I was holding my business (cock) smiling at him! I got my composure real quick, put my business away, and stood at the position of attention while I got reamed out by this man. My whole demeanor changed and I finally felt a sense of belonging. I tell you what, I felt at home from then on.

Two days later, we were picked up as a Company. Rudy and I were assigned to the same platoon but different squads. Let me explain how we were made up; there were four squads in a platoon. Each squad had a squad leader in charge of the four teams of four recruits. Each team had a team leader in charge of his team. So, there were 48 recruits to a platoon, plus one Guide. The Guide was our Platoon leader; he was picked by the Drill Instructors for his stamina, leadership, and marching skills. The Guide had to be able to carry the platoon staff, show that he was a good example to the rest of the platoon, and be able to march in a straight line, since the whole platoon followed him. It didn't take but one week and I was picked as a squad leader. I didn't know if that was good or bad for me since our platoon was a mix of assholes from all over the U.S. of A. One guy was from Argentina; he was barely in the U.S.A. six months and hardly spoke English. Another two were given two choices; either spend six years in prison or three in the Marine Corps. We had guys from Kentucky, Alabama, Tennessee, Wyoming, Texas, an Indian Reservation, and I don't know where this scrawny, coke bottle glasses wearing, 5-foot, freckled faced albino named Tucker came from! But he was our worst recruit of all! Even his voice was weird, it sounded like he had a nose full of snot! I'll get into Tucker later. We were always fighting among each other from the beginning to the end. Even when we were in competition with other platoons, we were our own worst enemies. Rudy, at one time, was ready to jump on one of the guys for talking shit to him. I got out there just in time to stop him as the Drill Instructor was about to walk out of the barracks. Oh! Let's not forget our beloved Drill Instructors; Sergeant Hammer was a white dude who did three tours in Vietnam. He had a habit of telling us Vietnam stories rather than read to us from the Marine Corps Handbook. He would have one of us recruits keep a watch out for incoming personnel while he told us stories. His main purpose was to teach us hand-to-hand and weapons tactics. He was the better of the three Drill Instructors we had. Then there was Sergeant Jackson; he was a black dude who did not see Vietnam but was very good at teaching us to March. He had that Marine Corps voice perfect for cadence; it was deep and loud, almost musical. His purpose was to teach us to March correctly and to have Rifle control while marching. Last, but not least, was Staff Sergeant Prick (that wasn't his real name), another black dude. He was the asshole of the bunch. He did one tour in Vietnam but wasn't as colorful as Sgt. Hammer. He just liked to try and bullshit us all the time. Once in the middle of the night he came into the barracks drunk and challenged us. He said he could kill any one of us with a Chinese Star (it's one of those things you throw) before you could shoot him from the other side of the barracks. He asked for a challenger. Of course, some of us knew he was full of shit, while others were scared to death! What a joke he was. Then there was the time he challenged me to a rope-climbing contest. Since I always made 300 on the Physical Fitness Test (PFT), I was the one to beat. Let me explain the PFT first; it consisted of 80 sit-ups in two minutes, 20 pull-ups, and the three-mile run in under 18 minutes. Each test was for 100 points covering the lower, mid, and upper torso. So my challenge was to get to the top of the rope poles using two ropes, one on each hand. As all the platoon was hollering and screaming for me to beat his ass, I proceeded to do just that! I beat him to the top and was on my way down with the platoon hollering and clapping because I kicked his ass real good. Then all of a sudden he flew by me (apparently letting go of the ropes) as I was going down the ropes.

He hit the sand below and rolled, hollering that he won! The Platoon got mad and tried to defend me saying the challenge was to the top, not to the top and bottom! He threatened to destroy all of us and we just figured we couldn't win and let him have his way. Next thing you know, we were all doing bends and thrusts in the sand till the sun went down.

All in all, I was in the best shape of my life. I went in weighing 128 lbs.; I came out of Boot camp weighing a very solid 148 lbs., plus I was very strong at 148 lbs. They (the Drill Instructors) had a new guy come in from another platoon (he had gotten into trouble and had to do a little brig time); he was a big strong black dude. First thing they did was try and intimidate me by telling me this guy was stronger than me and I was just a weak piece of shit like the rest of the platoon. Then they decided to test us by seeing who could do the most pull-ups. He went first and did 27; I stepped up to the bars and did 33. He tried again and only did 22; I stepped up and did 27. After that, I had his respect and no trouble from him. By the time graduation came around, I was so lean and mean they had to meritoriously promote me to Private First Class. I hadn't seen Victoria in over three months and she never looked so beautiful! Well if you read the last chapter, you know what happened with us. I really don't want to go there again, so let's just move on to my Marine Corps career. I was sent to Camp Margarita, top of the hill Margaritaville, home of the Second Battalion, Fighting Fifth Marines! That was where I got Company high on the Rifle Range shooting a 238 out of a possible 250 using an M-16 rifle. I felt very comfortable with the stretching and positioning techniques we were trained on in order to fire the rifle from 200, 300, and 500 meters. By the time the qualifications came around, I was ready, willing, and able to beat everyone there, which I did in an orderly fashion. I had shot all bull's eyes in the first two heats (200 and 300 meters). By the time I got to the last line (500 meters) I had a pretty big following including a Colonel, a Major, a few Captains, and my favorite top Non-Commissioned Officers. Well, the first shot was a miss way off to the left. Apparently, the wind picked up in the middle of the range and it didn't show on the flags at each end of the firing range. I adjusted my rifle and shot again and hit the outside of the target for another minus 5 points, which left me with a possible 240 high if I hit the rest at the bull's eye. I adjusted again; I had to make a calculated guess each time on my own, and I couldn't get assistance from anyone around me. So, I adjusted and shot a 3-pointer and adjusted again for the remaining bull's eyes and a top score of 238! I was the Company Rifle Range Champion, the best shooter out of 250 other Marines. That's what we called "Good Training!"

<u>August 1977, Oceanside, CA:</u> 1. Take vehicle w/o owner consent/ vehicle theft 2. Receive known stolen property.

While on leave, a couple of us Marines bought a used motorcycle from a local only to be caught riding a stolen motorcycle. We were cleared when our Platoon Commander verified we were on base at the time the motorcycle was actually stolen.

After about six months of being on top of Hill Margaritaville, I decided to go back to Sacramento and get my bike. That was one of the best ideas I ever had. I had a custom Honda 750. It was custom built to look like a Harley with the split big 5-gallon gas tanks, and the duel exhaust system, pull-back handlebars, and saddle bags. It also had a beautiful, clean blue paint job. I would go up and down the pacific Highway hitting all the beaches from San Diego, Ventura, Huntington, Malibu, all the way up to San Onofre. It felt so nice with the southern weather and the smell of the ocean and suntan lotion on all those beautiful suntanned babes. There were a couple of Marines who hung around with me; one was Corporal Mac from Missouri, another was Sgt. Ripton from Alabama, another was from Kentucky, and another was from an Indian Reservation. The two funniest were tall; one was 6'5" and the other was 6'6" and one was a white dude and the other the Indian. Then there was me at 5'7". We would go to town and get shit faced and raise all kinds of hell! Corporal Mac was fun, too! He had an old Rambler station wagon he thought was a four-wheeled vehicle. He would take that vehicle out in the boonies and get stuck almost every weekend. We all loved the best years of good old country music, like Waylon Jennings, Hank Williams, Jr., Johnny Paycheck, and Crystal Gayle, to name a few. We'd go to all the rodeos in and around base drinking and carrying on like we just didn't have a care in the world.

After a while, I got the Dear John phone call and decided to get as far away from Victoria as I possibly could. I kept wanting to go back to Sacramena and take her back, but I knew she was better off without me. So, I went overseas, first to Okinawa, then on a cruise to Hong Kong,

China for the 1977 Christmas, then to Pusan Korea for the 1977 New Year's celebration. After that, we went to my Marine Corps paradise, Subic Bay, Philippines! The town was nothing but bars, strip clubs, and places to eat and drink. There was little Texas, which was Philippine women, ½ Philippine and ½ white, dressed like cowgirls. They also had a little Mexico, little Puerto Rico, little Africa, etc. These bars, clubs, whatever, were filled with some very beautiful women who were ½ of one thing and Philippine. My favorite was a girl from the little Spanish area; I really liked her and actually took her on a road trip to Baguio. The trip was in an old dirty bus filled with chickens, goats, and little old Filipino people. It went along very steep cliffs with scary one-lane roads. By the time we got to Baguio, we were dirty, thirsty, hungry, and tired. Baguio was her home town, and she showed me the park where families lived in the park and took care of it. The town had a Tijuana type of atmosphere, everywhere were little vendors, yet it was very clean and relaxing, nobody was trying to get you laid or rip you off. It was a very relaxing weekend, until I finally tried to get a little piece of ass from her. At first, she kept making up excuses, then we sorta just did it. I think she was a virgin. We ended up walking and shopping, and having a good time. I really loved being around her. She had a lot of positive energy and I really needed that. But, when we got back to Subic Bay, everything went wrong. I had to go back to base for a few days and when I went back to town I tried to find her but she was nowhere to be found. The place she worked said she no longer worked there and they didn't know where she was. I was devastated; I really liked her. To this day, I still think of her and how if I had any children in this world it would be from her. I guess I'll never know. There was one more good story about the Philippines I should tell.

It was when we went on a forest march 22 miles into the deepest, darkest, most remote parts of the Philippines. We passed a giant lizard that stood on all fours and was close to 5 feet tall and over 12 feet long! It scared the shit out of me; the guide assured me we were ok as long as we left it alone. Later we passed a bunch of Black Pigmy people in a tribe-like setting with grass outfits on and holding spears, living in huts, just like they were in Africa or something. I'm telling you, this place was a trip! When we finally got to our campsite, it was so hot we were told to dress down and stay out of the sun and keep drinking water and salt tabs. We were done for the day, time to go exploring! We didn't make it but a mile and we heard, "Hey Marine!" It was our old ladies from the bars in town! They brought food, drink, and weed for us to party with. They even took us to a little waterfall. We got drunk, loaded, and were screwing these chicks in a circle fuck while each of us was rooting for each other to do it harder and longer, whatever made the most sense. Either way, we were a mess come morning time. We were all called to the company formation to take the march back to camp, or so we thought. The Captain said he heard that some of his finest Marine Corps Sergeants were out drinking and carrying on the night before and had neglected their duties by not staying close to camp and taking care of their platoons. Well, instead of beating the heat and leaving at 0600, we were to stay until 1000 and leave when the heat would be at its worse for the long march home. The march back to camp was a grueling 4-hour march through the jungle and then to the open road in the heat. The troops were dropping like flies; the heat was unbearable. As for the Major, he was really pissed and getting back at us the best way he could. By the time we got to the last hill, which was about a ½ mile up at a 30-degree angle, we were like dead men walking. Once all the platoons were gathered and in formation, the Major reamed us a little more, and called "At Ease!" We dropped right where we were standing and laid there for about a ½ hour before an ice cream vendor came by and started selling ice cream like it was going out of business.

We did some Jungle Environment Survival Training (JEST) while in the Philippines. It consisted of three days of classroom training on how to make fire, build protective living quarters, and find/hunt for vegetation and meat. Then four days of being in the jungle and surviving with a knife and the clothes on your back. By the time I was finished, I ate monkey, dog, cat, snake, worms, and fish along with some vegetation I will probably never see again in my lifetime. I really liked the training and the trapping and foraging. When we got back to Okinawa, we went on some cold weather training at the base of Mount Fuji. It was actually the back side of the pictures you see of Mount Fuji, the side no one knows about. We marched up to the rim of the snow cap and did some cold weather drills over the next 48 hours. I was never so cold in all my life; we slept in our fighting holes and basically did our whole training in and out of those holes for 48 hours, it was very miserable! When the big 6-by's came to pick us up and you could smell the diesel fuel, you knew we were on our way out of the shit hole. Even today, I get that Fuji Cold at times when I'm half-naked. It's a terrible feeling to be shivering and not able to do anything but curl up and try to warm up as quietly and swiftly as possible.

When I got back stateside, I couldn't believe the change in the camp. They had new rules in boot camp that the drill instructors could not scream, curse, holler, or beat (did I say that already?) the new recruits. I couldn't believe it! I talked with one of my buddies from boot camp (Rivas) and he told me not to become a Drill Instructor because I would lose my stripes in a day, with my bad temper and all. A few months later I was out of my beloved Marine Corps and riding out of Camp Pendleton with the song by Johnny Paycheck "Take This Job and Shove it!" playing loud and clear as I passed the platoon. I got my Honorable Discharge as a Marine Corps Sergeant in the Weapons Company, Dragon Platoon. Semper Fidelis "Always Faithful!"

When I first got out of the Marine Corps, I was hoping to get a job with PG&E. So I registered for the entrance exam and failed because I'm colorblind. Then I must have tried to get into the Pacific Telephone Company four different times until they decided to test me for a secretary's job just to get my foot into the door. I didn't make it past the written test. I stayed with my dad for a few weeks until I got drunk with some of the old Central Boys and tried to get back on my motorcycle and ride home. We were at Chita's place in Central and drinking up a mess, snorting lines, and smoking up the gangie. I was so stoned that Little Joe, a very large Piute Indian friend of mine, and I were trading stomach punches, or should I say punch. That big bastard hit me and I folded like an ironing board. After that I wanted to go for a ride on my motorcycle. They thought I was too stoned and pulled the plug wires on the bike so I wouldn't start it. I don't know how I did it but, I put them in just right and started the bike and was off and riding! I made it to within a mile of the house on Stockton Blvd. when I was at a stoplight revving up the motorcycle engine and looking all crazy drunk. As I took off, so did the police car behind me. I knew if I stopped they would take me in and either have my bike towed or left there (which was the middle of Oak Park). No way, I said and I was off and riding fast. By the time I reached my dad's driveway, there were three police cars and five policemen. I went to kick down the kickstand and miss it and the bike fell down on me. I was lying there with the bike on my leg and the cops with their guns pulled watching. My dad and Mano come out of the house and saw me lying there with the bike on me and the cops' guns pointing at me doing nothing. My dad yelled at them for not helping get the bike off me and for holding their guns on me. Mano and my dad pulled the bike up and helped me stand up. I turned around and asked the cops if they were taking my bike too. They said no, they just wanted me. So I put my arms out and went toward the Latin cop who was sort of smiling. I don't think the other cops would have been too kind to me. A few days later, I moved in with my brother Johnny in West Sacramena.

1979

I moved in with my older brother Johnny in a West Sacramena duplex. At the time, I was collecting unemployment and looking for a job. Instead, I had to start selling drugs (Cocaine) to make ends meet. I never did like the idea of selling drugs, it was just a way to make some easy money and party a little on the side, too. It was a lot of fun in the beginning as most new jobs are. I would buy my stuff out of town and have a packing party with a fine looking, young, blonde, white chick next door from us. She was a former Miss River City Queen. There would be her and a few more close friends there weighing, packing, and testing. My brother Johnny always had the weed and my Compadre Cesar had the crank. I liked the easy money, but the hours were getting to me. I had to stop selling after 10:00 pm or else these people would be calling all night wanting some stuff. You see, I didn't step or mess with the stuff too much like most dealers. I kept it as pure as possible. My prices were fair and the dope was great. A downfall for me was seeing a few of my customers get hooked on the dope and start selling their property and missing work and coming over all the time day and night. I stopped selling to them and advised them that they needed to go to counseling. They were my best customers and my worst. By them coming over all the time they were bringing attention to my operation. One of them eventually lost his job and his family within a year's time after dropping him as a customer. I was already out of the picture and he got hooked up with a scandalous prick drug dealer. The one thing I miss about the whole drug scene was the pussy and the fringe benefits! It was out there, everywhere you turned, if you had the dope. I had a few women who would invite me over or I would just drop by and we'd do a few lines and they would go down on me, or whatever I wanted. These were some fine women who had good jobs and nice homes, at least most of them were. Some would do other things for me such as cook, buy me clothes, or all the above. I got out when I caught myself getting stoned too many times in the week and spending more money partying than I had. It only lasted eight or nine months and I was out and about looking for an honest job.

I went to school at the Community Resource Project and got certified as a Solar Energy Professional (Solar Technician). The class was filled with really good training in electrical, solar utilization, plumbing, carpentry, and engineering solar panels. The people in the class were a nice bunch, too. We built a few solar panels and installed them in a few of the underprivileged areas of North Sacramena. The Solar Greenhouse we built at Sacramento State University was still up until 2005. That was also where I met and dated Roberta a few times. Roberta was a very beautiful, petite, smart, soft-spoken lady who had the prettiest little body and smile I'd ever seen. She was a counselor for the CRP and worked part-time as a maid to fund her law school studies. She actually came up to me and asked me out on a date. I was so surprised and excited. She wanted me to take her for a ride on my motorcycle. We did the ride and then I took her to my dad's house. We then went to my bedroom and she just started taking off her clothes and was on the bed waiting for me. I couldn't believe it! I didn't even have to try, beg, ask, or anything; she was willing and able to get past the awkward phase and get down and dirty just like that! She was an amazing woman from the start; I loved that woman. The only problem was she had a jealous ex-boyfriend she didn't want to leave. She also had a very smart son who was very respectable to her and who stayed with her full-time, not that it was a problem. Her apartment was very clean and fresh, nothing out of place and not cluttered. We didn't get serious and eventually just stayed friends. Roberta finally graduated, became a lobbyist, and bought a nice home in the William Land Park area. In her first year she made over $350,000 working out of her house.

1980

I start working for Texco Mechanical as a gas pipe fitter at Fort Ord. Roberta referred me to these people. Little did I know that these people were racist and drug addicts. The job was hard and long but paid good ($13.00 per hour) and we received all the drugs we needed to get the job done. We usually worked 14-hour days to stay ahead of the contracted amount per week and have the installations tested and passed before we could go back home that Friday. Friday early afternoon I would get back to the apartment to clean up and drink some tea with mushrooms for a nice trippy ride on the motorcycle back home. Back home, I partied with Mimi, Eli, and a few of her friends until I met Tonya. Tonya was a tall, pretty redhead, with a nice smile and long legs. She was also kind of naive and a big flirt. I had heard of her flirting and even saw a few picture of her with guys and just decided to have her part-time. We dated for a while, and when I started working at the Printing Plant, I moved in with Whitey. Whitey was a Harley riding, skinny, white boy, trash talking biker, he was a good guy though. Well, one day Whitey and I were talking about Tonya and how horny she was and that I bet she would do both of us. So, I decided to put her to the test and videotape her giving me a blowjob. Then I left the room and told Whitey what had happened and asked him if he wanted to have some of her when she got out of the shower. Of course he said, yes! When she got out of the shower and while she still had the towel on, I told her Whitey wanted to eat her box and would she let him. Of course she said, yes! So I took her out to the front room and sat her on the couch next to Whitey; he froze up and didn't say or do anything. I was just sitting there and inside I was cracking up because here was this big old biker afraid to make a move. After a few minutes, Tonya decided to go back to the room and get dressed; I just started laughing.

Tonya was working for PG&E and lived by Curtis Park when she was raped by a co-worker. Apparently, she was with a few of them having drinks and playing darts at a bar when they decided to go to a different place to party. This black guy with a corvette (that was Tonya's favorite ride) asked Tonya if she wanted to ride with him. She said yes and went with him to his house to do a few lines of coke first. When he got her there he shared some coke with her and started to rape her. She was scared to death and just froze as he took her clothes off her. He did what he wanted and got up to get some water, and she ran out of the house naked and was banging on a house where a woman answered. She called me to come pick her up. When I got there she was dressed in some clothes the lady gave her and scared. By the time I get to her house, the black dude had already dropped her clothes off on her porch. We called the cops and they asked her and me questions about how it came about. They said it would be very bad for her and the courts would make her out to be a coke addict and a flirt. She didn't want to press charges. Either way, the cops picked up the guy to ask him questions and more or less let him know he would be watched. The next day at work, the female employees were fucking with her about the rape charges and he was in there smiling at her. Tonya couldn't take it any longer and after a few days, quit. When I picked her up and was leaving the parking lot, I saw the black dude and another one standing outside their corvette smiling as we left the area. It was a few months after that I decided to quit seeing Tonya and told her so; she didn't take it too good. As I was leaving Whitey's house in the Arden Park area, she followed me across town to the William Land Park area. I was actually on my way to Lucy's house. As I drove into the Shell station on Sutterville Road and Freeport Blvd., Tonya ran into the side of my nice Cougar, knocking off a piece of the side molding. As she tried to get away in the gas station traffic, I jumped out of my vehicle, dove through her open driver's side window, and started beating her head against the door. She was screaming and hollering at me to stop! I kept telling her to quit following me and that she was going to pay to fix my vehicle! As I was leaving the scene, a couple of young ladies started yelling at me that I was such a big man for beating up on a girl. I got out of the vehicle and yelled at them that she was a nut case and she followed me from the Arden area and rammed my vehicle! They said something else that just pissed me off and I started to go after them, too! They ran a little and stopped when I did, so I left and they tended to Tonya.

Cleo is another beauty I dated and actually asked to marry me. I knew Cleo from earlier in my years through some friends in the Civic Circle area. Cleo was very nice, soft-spoken, gentle and kind, she had long black hair and was kind of naïve about certain things. I can remember her telling me about her dad and her talking about me asking her to marry me. Her dad told her if he was a woman, he would marry me. Cleo's parents were teachers at Sacramento College. They liked me and so did the rest of her family. That was another reason I wanted to marry her. The only drawback was a young girl she had from another man. Her child was spoiled rotten and I could not get close to her, and that was the straw that broke the proposal.

I met Sherry-Lynn through Cesar's niece Nicole. Sherry-Lynn was 18 years old and a strong, beautiful, German and French Creole young lady. Sherry-Lynn was built like a thick German with big tits! We liked to wrestle all the time for sex. She was strong (did I mention that before?) for a chick! What I liked the most about Sherry-Lynn was her attitude about people and things in general; she had a great attitude about life. I wasn't into much dope at the time but still liked to party and so did Sherry-Lynn. Sherry-Lynn and I dated off and on for a while. I asked her if she would marry me if I asked her. She said no because she was seeing someone else and didn't think it would be fair. Oh! Did I forget to mention that part? She was seeing another guy from school at the same time I was with her. He was a permanent college student from what I gathered. The last time I saw Sherry-Lynn was in 2004 at the Japanese Bizarre on Riverside Avenue and she was still going to college and dating the same guy from back in the day, had not married him yet, and still no children. She still looked great, too! We shared a few drinks and just caught up, and I never saw her again.

1981

At 25 years old, I started working at the Printing Plant, originally in the Pressroom, on the graveyard shift. I got a tip from Cat, my brother Nathaniel's kid's mother, about a job opening at the Printing Plant. The hours for the applications were from 8:00 am until 4:30 pm. I went around 10:00 am and the line was around the building and around the block. I left and came back at 3:30 pm and there was no line at all. I put in my application and a couple of weeks later, I was interviewed by a couple of guys who were former Marines and knew me from my earlier boxing career. Out of the over 250 applicants, they only needed 10, and I was number 10. I started in the pressroom on graveyard shift. I didn't mind the third shift time at all. I got used to it real fast since back then it was only seven hours per shift with a half-hour lunch period. I met a few old dudes who mentored me in the Printing Plant. One in particular was Bro who was better known to me as "Brother." Bro had been a pressman for many years before I got there. He was a small Latin man who was fun to be around, we would tell stories and joke around whenever possible. We enjoyed each other's company and I also enjoyed the way he would mentor me on the Printing Plant and the bullshit everywhere. I dated his daughter Angel much later in my career not knowing that she was his daughter at first. He didn't mind me dating her either since her husband at the time was a jerk and an alcoholic. Bro and I had a special whistle we did whenever we saw one another; we also always called each other "Brother." A few years after Bro retired from the Printing Plant, he got sick with diabetes and was bed-ridden for a while at home. I would visit him and stay for a while, and when I left, his wife Nellie always let me know how nice it was of me to visit since his other friends did not. Bro was finally sent to the hospital where he passed a slow and painful death. It was horrible! The hospital took him off the support system and for three days his family had to stay with him and vacuum out his saliva and watch him die. For three days! That was crazy! I miss my Bro and cherish our time at the Printing Plant.

June 1981-April 1982

At 26 years old, I started my boxing career again then retired for good at 27 years old. I came back stronger than before, knocking out four of the six opponents I faced. One of them I didn't want to knock out because he had fought Tiko, a friend of mine, a few months earlier and just beat Tiko all to hell. Tiko shouldn't have taken the fight but his handlers thought he should. Tiko was facing a guy who was a natural featherweight (126 lbs.) or at the least a big Bantamweight (118 lbs.). The kid's name was Vinnie. Vinnie beat up on Tiko from the beginning, he was just bigger and stronger than Tiko since Tiko was a Flyweight (108 lbs.). When I heard I could fight this Vinnie I went into some very intense training. This is the only fight I can remember where I wanted to hurt somebody, not just beat them up and win. So from the beginning of the first round, I took it to Vinnie and hurt him. Round after round, I kept beating on this kid. I let him survive each round playing with his body and mind, beating him down and letting him up. He staggered back to his corner more than once. I wanted to beat him for the ass whooping he gave Tiko, and I didn't care what anybody thought. I have to admit, Vinnie was tough. He stayed on his feet and kept coming back, and I was there to deliver. I should have and could have knocked him out at any time, but I wanted to share the pain he gave my friend. I think I got my point across when the bell ended and Tiko came into the ring and I told him the fight was payback for him. I fought a few more times and started to feel like I was wasting my time. The pay was still below average considering the time spent training. Even though I fought and won another California State Title, I just wasn't getting the recognition I needed to continue. Don't get me wrong, I had a nice following but they were not the big crowds most well-known celebrities or athletes had. I guess it was mostly my fault for the small shows. I didn't flaunt my boxing like some did by going out in the town and clubs partying or actively making my presence known in and around the town. I just trained hard and stayed close to my friends and family. In the end, I had a growth just below and between my nose and my upper gums preventing me from sparring before my last fight. After the fight, I went to the doctor because of the swelling around my nose and gum line. They took x-rays and blood work and told me I was lucky; lucky, because I didn't die from my injury while boxing. It was in an area of my face that if hit would have ruptured the blood vessel. It would have gone to my brain and I would have died from an aneurism. I was kind of glad I didn't die and that I wasn't fighting any more. I didn't want to have one too many fights and end up stupid or as they say "Punch drunk" or "Punchy."

1983

I moved to Cesar's place in the Citrus Heights area of town. It was behind the Birdcage Shopping Center at Sunrise and Farmgate Way. Cesar had a nice place with a swimming pool and nice female neighbors. Cesar and Evelyn's place was a party house most of the time. We would go fishing overnight and catch (well the other guys would catch) catfish and have a big fish fry the next day at Cesar's. The ladies would work on the drinks and veggies, and the guys would do the BBQ, drugs, and drinking. Cesar's neighbors to the west were two nice looking females who could have been lesbians or not. But, they would be in their backyard sunbathing naked most of the summer. We would have to sneak into the bushes to watch them because the bushes were so thick that was the only way to see. So, we couldn't just invite them over or they would know we were watching them. To the east was a young teenager who would run around her house naked or in her yard in a bikini. She was built to last, very nice and full of curves. Most of the guys were already hooked up with ladies except for a couple of us. We few would bring shapely women over to show off their bodies by the pool. The other ladies would get a little mad at us for doing that but we didn't care. Do you remember Tonya? Well, I brought Tonya and her sister Pamela over to one of the swimming parties. What a mistake that was! Pamela had big giant tits and wasn't afraid to show them off. She kept diving into the pool and her top kept coming off. She would stand up and her tits would be floating there for all to see. The guys would be staring and the women would be disgusted with them and me for bringing her. Then it happened. Evelyn (Cesar's wife) and a couple of the other ladies had to make a store run. A few minutes after they left, Pamela asked Cesar if she could use his shower because she had to get ready for work. Cesar said yes and showed her to the shower. Before he left the room, she was undressing in his shower that is in his bedroom. He locked the bedroom door behind him. He opened the shower door, got in with Pamela, got a blowjob and did other stuff to her. I figured he just had to push the envelope and was in the locked bedroom a little too long because Evelyn and the girls came home and she asked, where's Cesar? A couple of us guys were knocking on Cesar's bedroom door and trying to warn him of Evelyn when the girls returned. All of a sudden, Evelyn came down the hall toward their bedroom. We slowly stepped to the side and walked away. Evelyn was beating on the door. Pamela opened it up and was standing there in a towel while Cesar was acting like he was passed out all wet on the bed; he did put his clothes on but was soaking wet. Pamela grabbed her clothes and went to another bedroom to get dressed. Then she and Tonya were out the door. Cesar, still acting like he was passed out, was being hit and hollered at by Evelyn. He woke up and was looking at her like she was crazy. He asked her what the hell was going on? Evelyn was no dummy when it came to Cesar and his actions. They argued for a while; she just let it go and we continued to party. Finally, the boys and I got Cesar alone and got him to come clean with us. He was our Hero of the Month for that scene, what a stud!

I finally moved out and got a place on Marshall Way on the west side of William Land Park off Riverside Avenue. One of the most peaceful places I lived was on Marshall Way off Riverside Blvd. It was on top of a hill and a block away from the Broadway cemetery. The place was a duplex and was like new with new flooring and appliances. It came with a nice small backyard where I could grow nice small marijuana plants. My neighbor was a nice petite lesbian who was also quiet and never made any noise or had company over. I, on the other hand, would wash my vehicle in the front yard with the stereo blasting and every Sunday evening would sit on the porch and listen to Phil Gavant's Blues Radio Show, playing my harmonica after a few beers and a joint. The duplex had a small bedroom and was just perfect for a guy like me. My next place on 16th Ave. and Freeport was a two-story Fourplex on the east end of the William Land Park area. It was two blocks from William Land Park and three blocks from Sacramena City College. I lived in the upper studio with the big open pane window and a balcony. I really don't remember why I moved from the Marshall Way duplex, but I do know Marshall Way was the better of the two. This place on 16th needed a lot of work; the yard was dead, the studio I rented needed a new rug, the toilet needed to be replaced, and the air conditioner was shot. I eventually replaced or repaired all the above with the help from my friend Cesar. I had the Jeep Scrambler at the time and had to use it one time to pull out a tree stump. The damn stump snapped off and flew out towards my jeep and me almost hitting us. The neighbors thought I was a nutcase for doing that, but as usual, I didn't care. After a few months of living there, the place started looking nice and lived in. The yard was green and had flowers and a tree growing. I enjoyed keeping the yard landscaped. I also liked some of the other people who lived in the Fourplex. Especially the bottom neighbors, I could hear them getting it on all the time (she was a screamer!). I had my fair share of screamers coming and going, too. I enjoyed hanging out at the park playing basketball, walking, or running through the park kicking a soccer ball or just running.

CHAPTER 5

1984-1990 (29-35 YEARS OLD)

INTRODUCTION

These were the most turbulent years. I got back into boxing, won another California State title, moved onto drugs, biking, and partying with local motorcycle gangs, hunting, and fishing, all the while working. I feel I had a death wish; I didn't like people too much and knew I wouldn't make 40 doing what I was doing. 1990 was a big turning point in my life. At 35 years old, I was blessed with a three-day-old girl left at my doorstep who was my savior. For without her, I know I wouldn't have made 40.

1984

It had been three years since I started with the Printing Plant. At first, it was as a Permanent Intermittent employee working in the Pressroom (third shift). During the end of the first year, they sent me to the Bindery and I started my boxing career again. I got laid off and started working for another part of the Printing Plant called the Support Staff (SS) on Alhambra and S Street. My buddy from the Printing Plant Tony (he's Sicilian) and I started at the same time except he worked on the day shift. We were both laid off at the same time, too. The Support Staff had an opening because a few of the former employees were caught dealing and smoking pot on the premises. The timing couldn't have been better; Tony and I were running out of places to look for work. We went into Support Staff working as Machine Operator Trainees and were promoted to Machine Operators I's in no time. We did a lot of out-of-class work training on any and all equipment. Even when they brought in new equipment, Tony and I were the ones who would train on them first. We were pretty savvy machine operators, I'd have to say.

That's where I hooked up with Mimi, another married woman I dated. Mimi was a very beautiful woman with a very nice smile and long, brown hair down to the back of her knees! Her husband was a very tall (6' 5") Puerto Rican prick. He used to beat her up and abuse her just because he was a bully. I almost hospitalized him but Mimi talked me out of it because, as she put it, she didn't want her son to not have his Daddy. How stupid was that? We eventually drifted apart and just became friends. The crazy Sicilian friend of mine Tony ended up dating her after me. We actually talked a friend of mine Bobbie (a female Sicilian) into luring the tall Puerto Rican prick into the parking lot so we could hurt him. She even volunteered to do it herself, that's how crazy this girl was! Mimi decided to just leave him, which was a good decision on her part.

I ended up talking to my first wife Mary who was also married to a tall (6' 6") slim husband. Mary and her husband did not sleep together for almost a year before I took her in and tore her up! There will be more about Mary as we move into the next chapter.

When the Printing Plant's Bindery department had a few openings for Book Binder III's, Tony and I put in for them and got the promotions. We made $1,400 more a month with the promotion! Some of the guys at the Printing Plant were a little pissed that we got the jobs, but the Assistant Plant Printer explained to them that we worked out-of-class for two years to get the experience and deserved the promotions. That was the end of that! There were a lot of parties to attend and all or most of them were during or after work. The Printing Plant was very much into drinking and dope back in the day. Our Christmas parties were the best! Retirees would come and most of the Printing Plant employee's families would gather, too. There would be homemade wine, Everclear (it was a form of moonshine), Long Island Ice Teas by the water barrel, and other liquor and dope all over the place along with plenty of food! Some equipment would still be running but not a lot. We would party, pass out, wake up, and continue partying. Birthdays or retirements were fun, too! We would have strippers come in and put on a show. And it didn't matter if you were a man or a woman, we did not discriminate. Back in those days, everybody got along and we worked hard and with the utmost professionalism, if you can believe that. We were very proud of what we did and it showed when we were not partying. I hate to say this but it all went to the shitters when women started wanting equal rights to run the equipment and were filing discrimination suits. The next thing we knew, they were dropping dimes on our beloved Printing Plant and all the partying and strippers.

I went up the ranks pretty fast, as a Bookbinder IV, I operated the folders, gatheralls, mailing machines, cutters, Perfect Binders, and Muellers. Cesar and Evelyn had a friend named Lucy they introduced me to. At the time, I was still into the drug scene and so was Lucy. Lucy was a petite, beautiful looking, soft spoken, gentle, yet horny, Japanese woman. I loved Lucy a lot and always tried to show her. I loved Lucy's family, too; they were very kind to me and were traditional Japanese people. Lucy and I were inseparable for a while until the dope got the best of us and we had to stop seeing each other. I have very fond memories of Lucy and will not tarnish them with details about our time together. If I could do things over again, I would have never let her go. I still love that woman, and I'll always cherish our relationship.

Even though I quit dealing drugs, I did not stop taking them. Cesar and I were out partying one evening and ran into a couple of girls at a local bar. We decided to hit up a dance club with them. We had them follow us there in case they got stupid or we needed to get away from them. On the way there, I was stopped at a light and these two chicks ran into the back of my vehicle. I look into the rearview mirror and saw them laughing. You got to know, I always took good care of my vehicles and when I saw them laughing it up after hitting me I went crazy. I pulled into the parking lot of the club we were to stop at and looked at my vehicle; luckily, there was no real damage. But seeing the chicks still laughing it up made me even madder. I started to yell at them while they were still in their vehicle and they didn't care and started to roll up their windows. That was when I snapped and grabbed the driver by her collar and started slamming her head onto the side of the door and her window. Her friend was hollering and screaming. Cesar was cracking up; he couldn't believe I went nutty on these chicks for hitting my vehicle. Then he saw the bouncers coming toward us and said we should leave. I waited for the bouncers to come up and ask what was going on. I told them and asked if they had a problem with it. They didn't, so Cesar and I left them to tend to the chicks.

Little Joe was a big 300-pound Piute Indian and the friendliest guy you would meet. He could also be the meanest guy if you pissed him off. He had a girlfriend named Pinky who liked to get it on with two guys at a time. One night, when Little Joe and Pinky were no longer dating, Cesar and I went to her house and proceeded to have our way with her. She wasn't all that good but she did the trick.

Pito was a nasty looking Mexican with long, greasy, black hair and was built like a pear. He lived in a storage garage and rented two others on each side of the one he lived in. Pito was a local drug dealer and always had some drugs for personal use or partying. Pito was a lot of fun to be around because he always liked to party and always had the booze, drugs, and facility to party at. His two side garages were for vehicles and musical instruments. I would go there to party and work on my vehicle when need be. Once, on the way there, I saw this big-titted babe thumbing for a ride. I was in the Jeep with the top and doors off listening to some rock and roll. I pulled up to the chick and was feeling a little feisty. I asked her if she needed a ride and she said yes. I told her if she showed me her tits I would take her anywhere. She flopped out these big boobs onto my seat and I automatically started hyperventilating. I asked if I could touch them. She said yes just be nice. They were big and soft with plump nipples and just delicious looking. She asked if I could drop her off at her husband's shop around the corner. I said yes, dropped her off, and went directly to Pito's shop around the corner. I told Pito the story and he wanted me to take him to the shop, just to see the girl. I refused and just told him where it was. I love hitchhikers!

James was the President of the West Sacramena Lone Ones motorcycle club. James's son Junior worked for me at the Printing Plant. James and his club members frequented the Brick House Bar off of West Cap Avenue in West Sacramena. The Bar was a local dive and usually had a nice variety of clientele and biker chicks. It had one pool table and a stage for a band. The parking is great for motorcycles because you can see out into the two parking lots from inside the joint. James was a big Mexican with a great sense of humor when he was sober; when he was drunk, he was mean and funny at the same time. An example is when we were playing pool and he was making these lousy shots and getting madder by the shot. You have to remember this guy was the President of a motorcycle club known for their brutality and lack of conscience. Well, James got mad and started to push the pool table through the front door of the bar when he looked up at me. I was cracking up laughing and he stopped and started to crack up, too. Some of the other patrons of the bar were just looking scared and wanted to run. He stopped laughing long enough to ask a couple of the guys and me to help him put the table back. A little while later he asked me not to tell his son what happened. It sets a bad example for him he said. I agreed and we went back and ordered more drinks.

In this same bar, I was pulling up in my jeep and waiting for a couple of the guys to catch up when this biker chick I'd been eye-balling in the past pulled up next to me in her truck and asked me to follow her. I agreed and on the way out of the parking lot told the guys I'd be back. I followed this babe to her place off of West Cap Avenue. She lived in a rundown house with sheets for curtains and a dry lawn. When she opened the front door, she escorted me toward the back bedroom and told me this was her kitchen and it was where she cooked. I was still a little blind from the sunshine and just as I got my night vision, I could see her stripped naked and waiting on the bed. What a nice curvy picture that was. She was very well built and solidly developed. I had a hard-on before I got my trousers off! She started blowing me and mumbling that it tasted nice and that she was a one-man woman and that her man was all she wanted. She said his name and told me it was nothing, just a one-time thing. I was all for that, especially since she knew what she was doing. I let her get on top and she was humping and slamming her pelvis into me like she was exorcised, screaming and hollering like she was crazed. Me? I was getting off on her like I never believed I would. She must have had two or three orgasms before I finally got mine. I didn't want to wait there for more or for her man to find us there, so I cleaned up and left her lying there. I got back to the bar and my friends were worried for me since they knew her old man was a big mean bastard. I told them it would be alright. After that, whenever I saw her, we just smiled and I'd get a hard-on just thinking about our one afternoon soiree; she was one of a kind.

Stinky was another one of those guys who worked at the Printing Plant with me. He was also another drug dealer who liked to party. Our party place was The Pit on 16th Avenue in Sacramena. The bar was known for gamblers, dealers, and bitches. During the day, a lot of the older gentlemen would hang out, drink, and gamble. The evening would bring out the younger crowd that would hang out, drink, gamble, and deal their drugs for the nightlife partiers. The bitches would hang out and party with them all. The place was very small, enough room for one pool table in the middle of the room and in the way of everybody that passed through the doors. People still played on it and made just enough room for the person shooting to have room for their shot. Then like a clam it would close shut and this would happen all night. I must have gotten lucky a few times in their parking lot, especially when I had my van. We would go back there and smoke a joint or do a line and get it on real quick and head back to the party, nothing too personal though, just a quick thrill.

Tony was a short crazy, drunkard, Sicilian friend from the Printing Plant. We started at the plant together and moved up the ranks for a little while. We actually lived together, as I mentioned earlier. Tony got me into hunting both with a rifle and a bow. He even got me into fishing a little more than I liked. He definitely was not a good teacher, for sure because we hardly ever caught fish and never brought back a deer. We would mainly go to drink, do drugs, and get crazy. Tony liked to come back to the plant and tell everybody about the dumb things we did, and everybody liked to hear the stories. One time, we were hunting early in the season and we got drunk and passed out by the fire. The next morning we woke up covered in snow and freezing! We both raced to make a quick fire and start up the vehicle at the same time. Once we got warm, we started drinking and eating cold chicken and prepped for some more hunting. We decided to go to Reno that night and the thing was, whoever won the first $300, we were going to a Whorehouse and get laid. Tony won $400 and was not about to quit; he had a bad gambling problem and would not know when to stop. I took a little longer to get $350 and when he lost all of his money, he waited for me. He was not patient either; he kept bugging me to borrow money. I had to hold off, I wanted to get laid.

We left the casino and got to the Kitty Club in Laughlin at around 1:30 am and relaxed and had a few drinks while waiting for the right pair of ladies to arrive. We relaxed with the Madam and had a few drinks for about an hour or more until these two ladies came out. We knew right from the get go they were the ones. Mine was a beautiful, solidly built blonde; Tony's was a tall, long-haired brunette who looked Latin with real big boobs, too. We discussed the arraignments and decided against going in as a pair; I wanted to take care of mine all alone and personal. That was a very good idea on my part because mine was beautiful, smart, and fun. We did a few lines and smoked a joint and got it on like we were meant for each other. I ate her box and she went down on me like she knew exactly what I liked. I was making out with her and we were like new lovers having sex for the first time ever. We went over the hour and didn't care either. When we were finished we walked back into the parlor hand and hand, smiling from cheek to cheek. We waited for Tony and his girl to come out while having a few more drinks. You would have died laughing when Tony and his girl came out. They were both frowning and mad at each other. Apparently, Tony's girl had a guy before him that bit her nipples and so wouldn't let Tony touch them. Tony ended up grudge fucking her hard and continuously not being able to get a nut. I thought for sure they would be happy like my girl and me. Who would have thought they would have ended up all ugly faced? Did I tell you Tony liked to smoke, a lot? We were on our first hunting trip and were sharing a big tent. When in the middle of one of those cold nights as I was sleeping, I smelled this cigarette smoke and I started to get pissed and told Tony to put the cigarette out! He refused, so I pulled out my .44 Magnum, pointed it toward his side of the tent, and explained to him that if he didn't put it out, I would shoot holes in his side of the tent. He got the picture and went outside in the cold wearing only his chones (underwear) smoking his stupid cigarette. Another time, we were hunting and we brought along his nephew Sonny. Sonny and I were outside the tent shooting a popgun at paper ducks placed on the two cases of beer Tony brought. I wasn't doing too good at hitting these stupid ducks and decided to use a real gun. I pulled out my .44 Magnum and shot all the ducks and a few beers too. Tony came running out of the tent all scared and mad yelling at us for shooting his beer. I told him I shot the ducks too. We (Sonny and I) just laughed; Tony was still a little pissed.

Lyle was a handsome former football player and Printing Plant employee who got too deep into the drugs. At first, when he started working at the plant he was a genuine jock. He stood about 6' and weighed a solid 245 lbs. Most everybody liked Lyle; he was a very nice man most of the time. Lyle would go fishing with Tony and me. Sometimes Lyle and I would like to get physical with each other by wrestling or playing king of the mountain. He was strong and would manhandle me. I would keep coming back for more wearing his big ass down. He was a great fisherman and father to his two kids, until he met Ethal from the Printing Plant and they started dating. Ethal had just split from her husband and was dating me a little when Lyle first met her. I told him she was just a friend. Ethal liked Meth and drinking, so did Lyle, so they were a good pair. Lyle left his pregnant wife and two kids for Ethal. They later got married but were still doing the drugs and drinking. Both would come to work cut or bruised from beating each other up. After four or five years of this, they finally got clean and Lyle died less than a year later while watching TV with Ethal in the bed. He just dropped dead from a heart attack while Ethal got up to get a drink of water. She thought he was asleep and when he fell out of the bed, she freaked out. The last I heard, she went back to partying.

Wolfgang and Lynn are my daughter Toni's biological parents. They were another pair like Lyle and Ethal, always partying and fighting. When I first met and started dating Mary, she would take me to wherever her cousin Lynn was to party on drugs and drinking. For the most part, Wolfgang was a very fun guy to be around, always joking around. Lynn was the hustler of the two, always finding ways to make a buck. Wolfgang was a low key drug dealer and wanna be Devil's Own. A lot of the times we would meet at a bar on Del Rio Blvd that was owned and operated by the local Devil's Own motorcycle club. The club was cool about strangers like us and didn't hassle Mary or me. Wolfgang was living around the corner from his Mom (Ofelia) and was working on his truck brakes. When he finished working on them, he took it for a test ride around the corner. On his way back to the house, the brakes gave out and he ran right through the front room of his house. Luckily, no one was in the front room. He did some serious damage to the front of the house though. He got out of the truck unhurt and cracking up. Another time, Wolfgang and Lynn were at the same house and after a few hours of arguing, Wolfgang took off in his truck while Lynn was screaming and cursing at him. Wolfgang turned the truck around and was heading right at her standing in the middle of the street. He screeched to a stop within inches of her and she didn't even budge. They were crazy I tell you!

The bar whores at Tahoe Park Bar were another story to be told. I liked playing pool at the Park Bar and was a pretty good player, too. That's where I met a few of the local girls and we would end up in my van or in between the two buildings in back of the bar. I tried to have two at a time once; one of them didn't want it and backed out.

Cesar and I were at the Dos Coyotes Bar & Grill located off of Richie's Blvd. one night drinking and talking shit when a nice looking Latin lady walked in and jumped into our conversation. We didn't mind and we could tell she wanted one of us, so I stepped up to the plate and took one for the team. This lady was bragging about her new car, a Miata, which was a small two-door sport vehicle. She offered to take me for a ride in it. We made it around the corner, she stopped, and we started to make out. Before you knew it, she was giving me a blowjob and then pulled up her dress and slid me into her. We do this and the poor little vehicle was jumping all over the place. I was actually laughing at the way the vehicle was moving that we both stopped and laughed, then went back to the humping. This lady had a nice rack, too and loved to caress them. We got our pleasure and kissed for a minute and headed back to the bar. The lady left me in the parking lot, gave me her business card, and told me to call her. I never did.

Another time, Cesar and I were at the Dos Coyotes, we were walking in and greeted by a Tall Blond Bomb Shell. She definitely liked me and was buying us drinks and flirting with the two of us. When closing time came, she invited me to her hotel room, which was next door. We didn't make it out of the vehicle in her parking lot. She blew me, mounted me, we kissed and said good-bye. This Blondie had the nicest body, hard, yet soft skin, sweet smelling with an energetic presence. I was actually feeling her energy as we were together. I really enjoyed being around her; she was very good for my manhood. I met Cesar back at his house an hour later. Oh! The reason we didn't make it out of her parking lot was because her husband was inside the hotel room.

Cesar always liked inviting people from the bars he frequented back to his house. This one time, he had a couple of women with him. We (Evelyn, Cesar, me, and the two girls) were partying and I had to go to the can to take a leak. One of the girls followed me and offered to help. You must know me by now; I let her. After using the can, she started to jack me off bare handed. Then she got some baby lotion and did it some more. Well,

I was on a little crank, weed, and drinks, and it just didn't want to come like it normally would. So, she started to blow me. That didn't work, so she oiled up her ass and slid me in and that, my friend, did the trick. We were both moaning and groaning loud enough so when we were through and cleaned up, the people in the next room were cracking up. We both walked out of the restroom smiling and sweating. Cesar told me I owed him a blowjob for the past three girls he hooked me up with. I said OK, they were worth it; the next one was for him.

Pitts (a fellow Printing Plant employee) had told me about a biker bar named The Nevada Club and how it was a great place to play pool and meet biker chicks. So you know I had to check this place out. That Friday I decided to take the bike over to the Nevada Club; it was not too far from my place and sorta hidden in the back of a parking lot. So, I wanted to make a grand appearance and come roaring in fast yet smooth into the front of the place to park. The first thing I noticed was there were no bikes there. Either way, I got off the bike and proceeded to lock it up when I saw about five people from the bar come out and check out my bike. I got a few compliments on the bike from the guys and girls and then went into the bar and ordered up a shot of tequila and a corona chaser. I looked around and saw every one of them people wearing Harley shirts but no actual bikers. The place was a crank bar! Full of cranksters and wanna be bikers. It did have a few nice looking chicks in it though. So, I decided to wait for the first brave soul to come up and start a conversation.

She was a nice tight little blondie, wanting to play some pool. Little did she know I was a pretty good pool player, so I proceeded to kick her ass a few times and call it a night. The following week, I decided to check this place out again, only this time I took the van. It was a nice Black Panel Van customized to match the Harley and real clean inside. This time, the place was packed with more of the cranksters. I stayed for one drink and as I was heading out, this fine young chick comes running out and asks if I could give her a ride home. I said, of course I could give her a ride! As soon as she got in the van, she asked me if I had any crank and that she would do whatever I wanted for it. I said I did and no sooner did I say that than she took off her top and was showing me the most beautiful young delicious tits I had ever seen. I ain't kidding. They were beautiful and with full round nipples! I had to tell her to put those things away. We weren't even out of the parking lot and the people hanging outside were staring at us! Damn, she was young and beautiful for being a crank whore. We made it to her place and we parked a few houses from her apartment. I received a blowjob first then had her sit on it while I lapped those nice titties. Of course this was after giving her a few lines and the promises of letting her have the rest of the bag when we were finished. She was wonderful! I also think she might have been underage, maybe 18 or 19, either way, I wasn't asking, she was too sweet to let get away.

Bobbie, the crazy Sicilian mentioned earlier, was another nut case. She was short (5'0") but had a nice firm body and knew how to use it. Bobbie also had big titties for her size, and they were very sensitive. She would invite me and my buddy Cesar over to her house for drinks, food, and sex. Cesar and I would supply the drugs, smoke, crank, and coke, Bobbie liked them all. Once there, we would start messing with her, sucking on her titties and doing lines, drinking and fucking with her again and doing some more lines. Maybe we would take a break and drink a little and bullshit then back to Bobbie coming on to us by blowing us while the other watched or just getting us hard and sitting on it while screaming and wanting more! Did I tell you she was beautiful too? She had long Raven Black Curly hair and was a screamer. She couldn't get enough! She loved me to all hell and told me that anytime I wanted her to stop screwing everybody and that I wanted to have her to myself, all I had to do was ask and she would be my girl. It took a few days to think about it but when I decided to go for it I told her. So, I took her up on that offer and what a mistake! I picked her up for a dinner and a movie date night, you know, like happy couples do. Bobbie was wearing one of those very short black evening dresses that was form fitting and she looked beautiful yet nasty, very nasty! Her long black hair was shining, her lips were dark red, and her body was in full bloom. We almost didn't make it out of her house. I took her to a fine Italian restaurant and ordered up whatever she wanted including a nice bottle of wine. While we were sitting there relaxing and drinking our wine she started to undo my trousers and jacking me off under the table! She started to get more horny and the next thing I knew, she was under the table giving me a blowjob! Ya gotta know, I went with it for as long as I could until people started to notice the movement and the noises she was making under the table.

I had to damn near pull her up by her hair to get her up from under the table. I took one look at her and noticed she was all worked up and kind of scary looking, like a crazed person. We (I) hurried up and finish our meal and we were out the door. We finished what we started at a vacant lot a few doors down, or so I thought. When we got to the movie theatre and while we were waiting in line, Bobbie was wrapping her fine legs around mine and is humping me. I gotta say I was a little pissed because there were a lot of people in that line including young children! I grabbed her and told her in my firmest voice that she had to calm the fuck down! Once in the movie, again, I told her that were we here to see a movie and that afterwards we could have our fun. Believe it or not, we (she) made it through the movie. By the time we got to her place, she was all hot again and we went at it until the sun came up. I tried to keep up with her as best as I could but eventually had to sit her down and tell her that she was too much for me. We agreed and I continued to share her with our close-knit friends. My buds were happy to get at her again and I was happy for the break.

Loca was one crazy Mexican. I knew her through my brothers who dated her. Loca started working at the Printing Plant and before you knew it, we were drinking and fucking every chance we got. Loca was about 5' 2" with semi-long dark brown curly hair and big tits but a flat tortilla Mexican ass. That was ok, because she made up for it in her attitude and her blowjobs plus she was a good-looking women. She acted all tough and mean, but behind closed doors, she was a pussycat. She did whatever I asked, including taking out her false teeth and giving me the best blowjobs ever! We had a pact though. It would have to be in the dark and I would not be able to see her without her teeth in, to which we both unanimously agreed. She also had a very weak sexual position that I found to be very stimulating for her. I would raise her left leg up and put it on my shoulder while sticking my cock deep inside of her. It went all the way in until it hit something and that was the spot! She would scream, holler, scratch, and bite. I would love to have that much control over her and would nut up like a mad dog! The one problem about Loca was that she could not drink too much. Our drink was mainly Bacardi (rum) and coke. I could tell when she was having too much, she would start to get mean and loud, sort of bordering the fence of either being real horny or fighting mad. I really liked the horny side of the fence but when she crossed over the fence to the other side, I usually left her hanging; it was either that or sock her. She would get all belligerent and loud and throw punches and slap at me for no good reason at all or want to tell me how much she loved me and for me to tell her the same whether I meant it or not. If I didn't, she would want to fight. Eventually, I left her and started dating other women and she started dating other men from the plant.

Catie was a silly White girl from the Printing Plant too. Catie was at first married to a nut case, then started dating a nut case, and then we started seeing each other on the sly. I didn't want anyone to know about us because her Dad worked with us and was a very nice man. He had issues with his daughter and the men she chose to be with. I didn't want to add to his list of men to dislike. Catie and I would meet at my place for a few drinks and some boom-boom then I would kick her to the curb. Nothing serious, she was too ditsy for me. Besides, she wasn't all that good under the sheets. I would have to say that she was a girl in between girls for me. She eventually hooked up with another Printing Plant employee who was a supervisor and they settled down and got married and they are still together, both retired and happy.

Thunder Thighs was a voluptuous White girl I dated from the Printing Plant for another very short time. We liked to snort coke, drink, smoke weed and get crazy under the sheets or wherever we could. Once she got caught blowing me at Tony's house in the front room. We thought Tony was asleep, but I guess he wasn't. He walked into the front room and I was standing up with my drawers down getting head from Thunder thighs. She stopped long enough for Tony to look and leave. By the time he turned around to leave she was up and sitting on the couch like she was innocent. Thunder Thighs later became our Superintendent in the Bindery. Thunder Thighs also started getting real fat and our escapades turned into a running joke with the boys and some of the girls.

Li'l One was another employee at the Printing Plant I dated. Li'l One was 4' 11" with a nice round ass, and big round tits (40s)! Li'l One had soft skin, a big smile with natural red lips, and long thick brown hair. She was also one of the loudest screamers I ever dated. I would barely have it in her and she would start screaming and getting off. There were times when I had to cover her mouth with my hands or a pillow to muzzle her up. Her daughters heard her one time and came running upstairs banging on the door thinking she was hurt. She told them that we were playing and that she was alright. Li'l One's kids (two girls) both loved me because I was very kind to them and paid attention to them when they needed it. They were kind, quiet, attentive kids that needed loving from a father figure and I enjoyed being that guy on 16th Avenue. The one significant thing about this place was what happened to me one cold winter night. I was dating Li'l One and was about to kick her to the curb for getting way too deep into the drug scene. (You have to know that I usually have a backup babe before I kick a chick to the curb.) Li'l One was nice and shapely but had an attitude. I was starting to talk to Mary a little more seriously now; so after a few days of hunting with Tony, I had her visit me at 16th Avenue. Li'l One didn't know I was back yet and happened to see my Jeep in the yard. Li'l One was knocking on the door and talking to herself saying; is he OK? Maybe he's passed out. Maybe he's hurt. You know, stupid shit like that. Mary and I were inside the studio staying quiet hoping she would go away. All of a sudden, Li'l One was breaking into my studio. I opened the door and could tell that she was all tweaked out on Meth. I asked her what the hell she was doing and to get the fuck out of there. She saw Mary in the studio and started to cry and yell at the same time. I grabbed her and escorted her off the porch and to her car explaining to her that she was a tweaker and that was not what I wanted or needed right then. Li'l One knew me pretty good and knew better than to do anything stupid and just sat in her car for a few minutes and left. Mary and I eventually moved in together, and that is another story to be told later.

I got into my new home on 10th Avenue in Tahoe Park circa 1989. As you know from before about Tahoe Park is it was a nice place to grow up, and when I was able to find and buy a house close to my Dad, I jumped on it. The house was a small two-bedroom place with one bathroom, a small dining area, and a rather large kitchen. The front and back yards were small and it had a small detached garage. The house was made of cinderblock and also had a nice brick fireplace with an insert. The first thing I did was have it painted by my friend Cesar. Then I started planting some trees in the front and the back, white birches and redwood trees. It also had a nice big Jacuzzi in the back patio.

1987-89, On and Off Mary

I met Mary when I worked for a few years at the Printing Plant's support services branch along with Tony. Mary was the Support Services Chief's secretary. She was very pretty, soft spoken and a lot more. I have more about her written in the next few pages when I talk about my adopted daughter Toni and my first marriage.

1990

At 35, I had one of those significant emotional events that would change my life forever; I adopted a three-day-old little girl. I was 35 years old. It was time to get cleaned up and raise a daughter! Her name is Toni, and she was a three-day-old ½ German, ¼ English, and ¼ Indian, blond-haired, blue-eyed little girl when she was brought into my home. At the time, Mary and I were seeing each other again and actually lived together. We were a couple off-and-on for over five years when she moved out. Mary was living in San Carlos, CA, which is in the Bay Area, when the big San Francisco earthquake hit in 1989. She got scared and needed to move back to Sacramena. I decided to let her live with me until she could find a place of her own. Mary and I were living with each other on 10th Avenue in the Tahoe Park area of South Sacramena when her cousin Lynn gave birth to Toni.

Let me explain Lynn a little more. Lynn and Wolfgang were bikers who loved to party with the Devils Own bike club and other bikers. They often partied on drugs such as crank and pot, booze, and whatever else they could get their hands on. While Lynn was pregnant, she still partied. After three days of testing Toni and her Mom Lynn at the hospital, it was concluded that Toni was born a drug-baby; she had crank (meth/speed) in her system. They came to my house where Lynn slept for a few days, then left. When Toni was placed in my arms at three days old, I knew she would be safe because I knew right then and there I would protect her from the life she had waiting for her if she went with Lynn. Lynn agreed to leave Toni with us and even wrote a letter to that effect. Wolfgang was already in a bad way from getting attacked at one of the local biker bars by his house in North Sacramena. He had a hatchet stuck in his head and an ice pick in his back when they found him (rumor was, Lynn planned the attack to collect the insurance, except Wolfgang did not die). Wolfgang was never the same; he ended up with a limp and a mind of a 12-year-old. As for Lynn, she went on a partying binge and would only show up to take Toni to her house when the welfare workers came by. This way she received welfare money for having Toni. This went on for a few months until I found out she was leaving Toni with drug addicts or alone in her swing while she was out partying. One afternoon, I decided to stop by Lynn's house while she had Toni. I found my little girl all alone in her swing sleeping. I packed her bag and took her home.

That was when I decided to marry Mary and get full custody of Toni. I have to admit, I hadn't stopped all the drugs and partying I was doing, mentioned in the previous chapter, even though I did back off a lot. But once I decided to be a full-time Papa, I quit all the drugs, partying, and sold the Custom Harley (1980 80" FLH), the Custom Van, and the custom truck. I eventually bought my first domesticated vehicle: a white, four-door Chevy Corsica. The way I looked at it was, if I were to adopt a white baby girl, I would have a better chance if I had a white wife. Even though Mary was a very good housekeeper and cook, she still had a drug problem. But I had no choice, and we got married. It was kind of funny when we were in the Child Protection Services (CPS) courtroom. Mary and I were telling the court privately how Lynn had a bad temper, was very vengeful, a drug addict, and hung around dangerous drug addicts and bikers. It was hard for the court to see this, especially since Lynn came in dressed like a nice, clean, church person (Lynn was a natural beauty anyway, she had long, blond hair, a beautiful body, and a clear complexion with bright white teeth). Lynn was no dummy either, she knew how to work the court until Mary said something about her past that just set Lynn off! Lynn started yelling and cursing and threatening Mary with bodily harm! I just looked at the judge with a smile on my face and told him that this was the Lynn we knew. It didn't take long for the judge to declare that Lynn was unfit as a parent and give Mary and me sole custody of Toni. We all agreed Lynn could see Toni once a week for an hour under our supervision and money was not needed; I would take sole responsibility of Toni's care, including her health and dental coverage. Lynn could only see her one hour per week at our location and under our supervision. Lynn was super pissed but couldn't do anything about it. She had a son a few years older than Toni named Robert. She had to be cool or else she could have lost him, too. After a few months of this arrangement, Lynn stopped visiting Toni and didn't come around for years.

Ok, back to Toni. I took a child psychology class at Sacramena College that helped in my child-raising abilities. I also inquired about the child being born a drug baby and learned even more. For one, I was to keep her wrapped up tightly and keep her close to my heart to keep her calm and make her feel loved and safe. So, every day I would come home from work, pick up Toni, and wrap her up and have her lie with me while I took my nap before I headed for the gym. Again at night, I would wrap Toni up and have her sleep between Mary and me. I took her everywhere with me, such as the gym, walking, while doing yard work, everywhere. She was a very loving, warm, beautiful, happy baby. She slept through the night and took naps pretty easily during the day.

Mary was a great Mom, too! Mary was still doing drugs but she was always on top of Toni's care. I loved being able to raise her as my own, and my family began to love her as well. Eventually, when Toni was able to walk, I would take her over to the Boxing Gym with me; you see, she went everywhere with me. We were inseparable. The first few days were scary for some of the fighters because Toni would be playing in the gym and running around and a heavy bag would hit/bump her and she would get knocked across the room. The fighter would be all scared that he had hurt her because she would be crying. I would just dust her off and tell her she had to be more observant of her surroundings. This happened a few times before she got her vision down and it didn't happen again. As she grew, the gym was like a big playground. She would climb the bars that held the heavy bags, wrestle in the ring, jump rope with the boxers (both male and female), and actually started working out with some of them and doing our exercises. The gym was a fun and healthy environment for her. We even had a curse can in the gym for those boxers who cursed a lot. If you cursed when Toni was in the gym, you had to put a quarter in the can. Toni didn't wait too long to figure this one out. She would tell stories about each of us and got us to cursing (all in fun!) and we would have to pay up. Toni was a little hustler even back then.

I believe even to this day we were meant to be together. I was at a place in my life when I didn't care who I hurt or what I did to myself or others. I did not believe I would make 40 years old and I had a death wish; this I firmly believed! But when Toni was placed in my arms and I held her and looked at the fragile little baby girl, I knew it was my calling to bring her up and save her and myself from all the evil out there knocking at our door. Therefore, I believe we saved each other and would always make sure we were safe and protected. Mary and I stayed together another year or so. Our time together was very violent or loving, depending on the drugs we were on at the time or the lack of drugs. We were both hot-tempered and fought a lot or were making love a lot. So, when she went to drug rehab for the second time and ran away with one of the drug dealers, that was when I decided to get a divorce and make Toni's life as safe and sane as I possibly could. This is where the adventure began. I got to read and see things I never knew as a kid. I was brought up a lot differently. I loved being Toni's Papa. I would still take her to her Oma's (Ofelia) house (where her Dad lived) at least every other weekend. I wanted to make sure she knew her Dad. Her mother never came around for a long time (maybe once a year, if that).

Grandma Mary lived across the street from us on 10th Avenue. Mary had a Grandson named Jonas who was a few years younger than Toni. I would take Toni to Mary's house in the morning (5:30 a.m.). She would take them to school and I would pick them up after school (3:00 p.m.). It was a nice arrangement that lasted until Elizabeth moved in (see the Elizabeth chapter) in 1999. I let Toni do all the things most parents didn't let kids do, such as play in the rain, climb trees, run in the house, and sometimes jump on the bed! I wanted her to live the life of a child, and have a fun and loving relationship with life in general. Toni in turn would bring me flowers, draw me beautiful pictures, make me laugh all the time, and bring such love and joy to my heart I thought I would explode.

When she first learned how to ride her bicycle, she started with training wheels. She didn't like them and we practiced riding without them while I held on to the seat running up and down the block. Finally, I let go and she did fine knowing I was holding on until she looked behind and saw I was not there; she panicked and ran into a bush. I almost wet myself. She was mad at me for a minute, then got back on the bike and was done with the training wheels forever. That's another thing we had going for us, we could and would never stay mad at each other for over a minute. It was so unique. If she got mad at me, a minute later we would just pick up the conversation where we left off, no questions asked. To this day we are the same, except we will sometimes talk about what made us mad and how to get over it, should it happen again. What a wonderful relationship we have. I always made sure she had what she needed and sometimes what she wanted. Toni was into drawing, so I made sure she always had everything she needed to draw or color, easels, crayons, paint, pencils, chalk, paper, etc. She also loved for me to tell her a story at bedtime; I would tell her a (clean) story about me when I was growing up. Then I would give her a kiss goodnight and tell her I loved her (I still do except for the story part).

The few women I dated loved Toni because she was such a beautiful, sweet, and behaved little girl. I would always get compliments on her manners, except for a few times. At the Dr.'s office, I had told Toni earlier not to say "fat people" when talking about big people; she was about six years old at the time. We were in a doctor's waiting room when a very heavy woman came out of the doctor's examination room. Toni looked up at her and in her little voice said, "Gee Papa, she's big!" Well, it was loud enough for not only the patient to hear but for the other people in the room to hear. Some of them kind of chuckled while others, including the big woman, gave both of us a real dirty look! I gave Toni a mean look and she started crying and said sort of loudly, "But Papa, I didn't call her fat!" I had to take Toni outside and explain to her that she should not have said anything. When she was finally done crying and we had our composure (me not wanting to laugh, and Toni not wanting to cry), we went back in to a very quiet waiting room. One lady did try and lighten up things a bit by telling us (very quietly) of an experience she had that was similar to ours. It helped a little.

The hospital experience was the first and last time I ever spanked my little girl. We were at the hospital visiting my niece (Danelle) when she was having her first child. Toni was about seven years old. We were on our way out of the hospital when we were passing the concession stand. Toni and I had a thing about buying stuff; we would go in, get what we wanted, pay, and leave. That is what we did, and it worked for us. Well this time, I told her the usual hurry up and get what you want and get it up here. She kind of looked around for a few minutes, so I gave her a one-minute warning.

She didn't comply and I told her we were done. I started to walk away and she began to throw a fit, yelling, screaming, and telling me she wanted to go back and get the candy. By then, we were outside the hospital and people were out there smoking or waiting for a ride, watching this little girl act crazy and spoiled. I told her in her ear that I was going to the car and if she did not want to come I would leave her. She decided to stay and holler some more as I walked away. By then, I was a little distance away from her and she started to run toward me, while people were just watching us carry on. Toni caught up to me and was crying. I told her in a soft, yet firm voice, that I was going to spank her ass when we got home, and that I was so mad at her that she should not talk to me. The ride back home was very quiet. She tried to be funny and break the silence like we usually did when we were mad at each other; it didn't work. I was so mad I couldn't even talk. We got home, I opened the door, she took one step in the house, and I grabbed her and spanked her ass two times hard! Then I sent her to her room crying. About a half hour later, I had a talk with her to explain her actions and how she made me feel in front of all those people. Toni, being the bright girl that she is (even if she is only 7), understood and never did that again.

I always tried to make her happy because that is how she made me. We were together forever, and we knew that. One of my most memorable Christmases together was when we were at Macy's with Mary and looking at some wooden horse teeter-totters. All of a sudden, I heard a squeaky noise coming from behind me and it was Toni on a wooden motorcycle just going as fast as her little legs could take her through the Macy's aisles. She was so happy and having so much fun, I decided to get that for her main Christmas present; I still have it at the house in very good condition, too!

Did I tell you about her climbing skills? Toni was one of those kids who knew no fear; she was also one of those kids who could out-climb most of the kids in the neighborhood. Our block had a lot of kids on it and they would do the kid thing and climb trees. One day I was coming back from the store around the corner and I heard a voice coming from above. I looked up and saw about five kids (three girls and two boys) up there and they all started laughing. As I was looking up, I saw Toni on the highest branch hanging like a monkey. I calmly informed them that they should get to the other side of the tree that was over the lawn, in case they fell. That way they would land on the lawn, not the sidewalk or street (they listened).

We had a cat named Tigger; she was an unusual cat (like most of our pets). Tigger was Toni's first cat and her most memorable; she took that cat everywhere. Tigger was very good with her. She could dress it up, drag it around everywhere, put it in her wagon for a ride, and let other people play with it as well. This one time, our neighbor Lisa had her parrot on her shoulder in the front of our house. The kids were just sitting on a blanket drawing and snacking. So, the kid put the parrot on a branch of a small Redwood tree we planted that year. All of a sudden, out of nowhere, Tigger ran up and grabbed the parrot in its mouth and started chewing! The kids were hollering and Tigger started running, chewing, and running some more! My future step-son Joe and I, along with Toni, Lulu, and Lisa started to chase the cat! Joe and I went one way, the cat with the bird in its mouth went the other. Tigger was running toward the backyard and we chased it one way while the girls went the other. Tigger stopped long enough to take a few more bites and ran the other way, leaving a trail of feathers behind. Tigger eventually dropped the parrot and took off. The poor parrot was half chewed up and we (Joe, Lulu, Toni, and Me) were just cracking up. Lisa was sad for her parrot and went home where the parrot died in the next few hours. I'm telling you, I never saw anything like it! Tigger did not discriminate either; it brought home a live baby squirrel, quite a few half-eaten mice, and a lizard (minus the tail).

Ok, back to Toni. She was very good with animals and young children all her life. We talked about her being a child psychiatrist so she could have her own ranch with horses, dogs, cats, chickens (chickens were my idea), a pool, and a complete kid's recreational area. I would have a nice little cottage in the back and take care of the property and she would be the doctor (psychiatrist). Toni went to David Lubin Elementary School and loved the monkey bars. She loved them so much I received a call from the school principal one day. The principal wanted me to have a conference with her and Toni right after school. I got to the office and noticed my little girl crying. Right off, I was going into Papa mode and was ready to kick some ass! Then the principal walked out and handed me a note from the school nurse. The note was to inform me that Toni could not play on the monkey bars until her hands healed. I looked at Toni's hand and I was shocked to see at least five or six blisters on each hand. Toni cried and said they didn't hurt. I felt really bad for her and explained they may not have hurt but they could get infected and make them worse. She understood and we left the school to get ice cream to make things better.

Our first trainride and Disneyland trip was a blast! Toni was around six years old at the time. I had already booked the trip with a trainride to Disneyland. It came with a hotel room across the parking lot from Disneyland. Included in the trip was the Disneyland breakfast package with the Disney characters. We packed our clothes and headed for the train station in Sacramena. From there, we took a bus to Stockton, a train, a bus, another train, and a taxi until we made it to Disneyland and our hotel. In between the bus and train rides, we had to carry our bags, hustling to get from one ride to the other. It was fun and Toni was the perfect child. When we got to our hotel, we cleaned up, I took a quick nap, we ate, and we were off to explore Disneyland. We had a lot of fun our first day. We stayed up late to watch the end-of-day light show and parade. We got up early the next day to have the breakfast special with the Disney characters. The rides were fun except Toni was not quite tall enough for some rides and that limited our experience. There were still plenty of other things we could do. Shopping, eating, and playing games all day was very tiring, but it didn't stop us. We kept going each night until closing.

The following year we decided to try something different. We would get up early on a Friday and leave for Half Moon Bay to do some horseback riding; Toni always loved horses. I even had her in some horseback riding classes at the Crazy Jack Riding Stables in Jacksonville. She would learn to bring in the horses from the pasture, clean them up, saddle them, as well as how to ride. At the Half Moon stables, we would ride a horse pre-picked by the staff according to our horse-riding abilities. The horses were old and a bit cantankerous. The one I had was part mule; it was so stubborn. I will bet a bottom dollar that if someone had been filming me ride that horse, I would have been able to win $10,000 on *America's Funniest Home Videos*. I'm not really a very good horse rider and this horse seemed to know it. On the way back to the stalls, my horse started to gallop. I was behind everybody (thank goodness) sliding back and forth, going up and down in the saddle and sideways. I tried to get my composure and hold onto the horn of the saddle and I was all but falling off. I finally got the damn horse to stop. I got my composure and rode smoothly back to the stalls. When we got back to the stalls, we relaxed and had a burger and some fries and started for Santa Cruz beach and boardwalk.

We got to Santa Cruz and our hotel at about 3:00 pm. We rested, then started for the Boardwalk. Toni was at an age when she was too tall for some rides and too small for others. We spent most of our time on the beach or along the piers shopping and eating. That night, the inside of my legs were bruised and sore from that damn mule I had.

Watching my daughter grow further and further away from me as a teenager...

I knew from experience and reading that when Toni hit the teenage years, she would change for better or worse; I got a bit of both. In elementary school (Lubin), she was very active with all the kids and was always happy to see me when I would pick her up from outside her classroom. She would tell me about her friends and their day, and I would listen and laugh at all the fun stuff she would experience during the day. Toni was tested academically, and they found out she was very gifted. They wanted me to enroll her in the gifted classes and have her come to school early and stay late to be all she could be academically. I thought about it and saw some of the other gifted students and decided not to subject her to that curriculum. The kids had no life after school; they didn't get to grow up being a kid. Sure, they will be successful (maybe) and make big bucks when they grow up. But they didn't get to be kids when they were just kids. I even asked/discussed it with her, and we decided that as long as her grades were A's or B's, we would not worry about it. But if she started getting bored with schoolwork and got lazy, I would stick her ass in the gifted classes and she would never see sunlight again until she was an old lady!

I especially enjoyed the plays and events the school would have at the school. She was a very talented athlete, too. She could throw the football or baseball better than most of the boys. She could even play basketball and baseball better than them, too! The school had a special place for special kids who were disabled. Toni was able to learn sign language, interact with these students and showed an ability to understand and work with them. This is one of the reasons I thought she would be an excellent child psychologist. Everything was great until she hit the Junior High School age and was changed from my little tomboy to a teenager!

Sutter Middle School was just around the corner and a few blocks from David Lubin Elementary School. The school was rated the best public middle school in Northern California. The school recognized her talent and since we still didn't want her to go to the gifted classes, she was enrolled as an office assistant during one of her periods. Right off the bat, she had to deal with being the freshman class. There was a lot of peer pressure, adjusting to the dress codes and latest fashions, and the boys! Between her personality and her beautiful looks, she was a hit with the young and older groups. She fit in real well at her school but started to get a little too fashion trendy. In the beginning, she had still liked to ride her skateboard and be the tough basketball playing girl.

As the years went by, she ended up wearing make-up, dressing in the more trendy outfits, and getting a little stuffy, if you know what I mean. Then she went from a straight-A student to a solid-B student. I could live with that. She was still a good kid, especially since it was during her middle school years that I went through the divorce and she had to actually take a few busses to get to school from the house we had on La Riviera. She was a pretty good sport about it and made it safely to school and back every time. I was very proud of her for being able to step up to the plate and girl-up. However, at home it was a different story! She had her own room, nice new furniture, new everything after the divorce. But, she was a slob! We sat down and discussed her lack of cleaning and came up with this plan: as long as her grades were at a B average or above, she cleaned the house each week respected and the house and me. I would give her $50 a week and not worry about her private space. This went pretty well until she started leaving the rest of the house a mess too!

West Campus High was another very highly rated public school, mainly known for its academics not its athletics. I'll get into that in Chapter 8.

CHAPTER 6

1991-1997 (36-42 YEARS OLD)

INTRODUCTION

I got married, off the drugs, divorced, and away from the entire bad, negative, no good people I had surrounded myself with, leaving me with a daughter to raise. It didn't take long before I divorced my wife who was on drugs and ran off with another man in drug rehab. Then my Dad had a stroke and I started running the gymnasium, raising Toni, and training Leroy. I got promoted and then discriminated against at the Printing Plant.

1991, I got married and quit drugs and partying all together.

Some people (mostly women) think of how their marriage will be; I didn't. So, when I decided to get married for the sake of getting custody of Toni, it was really no big deal. Sure, I loved Mary; we were just too drugged up most of the time to really live the life of a happy married couple raising a baby girl. We tried, or at least I tried a little harder. When we got married (I don't know the exact date), we were pretty stoned. What I do remember about the wedding goes like this. It was raining as we drove to Reno. Mary's mom and dad, her grandparents on her dad's side, and a couple of their friends met us there. Mary and I were getting stoned (wired) on the way there, during, and after the wedding. In Reno, it was snowing, not hard but snowing enough to cover the roads with snow. We drove the custom black van I bought from Mary's dad Tom. Mary and I were arguing a lot during the whole weekend. Even after the wedding when we were done partying and back in our room we argued. In fact, we argued so much we didn't even consummate the marriage by doing the deed. She was tweaking and running her mouth so I went to bed alone to sleep. The next morning, I jumped on top of her and fucked her! I told her it was official, then got up and showered, which pissed her off all over again. I tell you, it was a horrible way to be all the time. On the way home, we get stuck on the freeway and were told we had to turn around because of the blizzard ahead. At first, I thought how fucked up it was until we ended up back in Reno at a Fantasy Inn Hotel. The Fantasy Inn had a heart-shaped bed with mirrors on the ceiling, a Jacuzzi, and shag rugs. We got wired, loaded, and had a few drinks while waiting for the Jacuzzi to fill up and the bubbles to fill. I guess we waited too long and got too stoned and flooded the place with bubbles. We didn't care; we still had fun watching porn flicks and boning all night, at least six hours! The next morning, we were feeling a lot better about the marriage and had a nice ride home. It became evident that we had to quit the partying just by the way we were treating each other. I just stopped one day but Mary didn't.

I ended up taking her to a drug rehab center where she got clean and was back to the Mary I had fallen in love with. Mary was a very clean and nurturing person, always kept the house clean, her body sweet, and always had food cooked and ready when dinnertime came around. Mary was the best cook I ever met. She always made a big dinner or meal with all the fixings, plus desserts. I finally knew what it felt like to be happily married and raise a family. I even sold my Custom Harley (1980 80" FLH Harley) and the custom van and bought a four-door Chevy Corsica painted white with a small six-cylinder motor. Dammit! Talk about being domesticated! Everything was going great; I even got promoted to Supervisor at work and let Mary know she didn't have to work; she could just stay home and take care of Toni. What a big mistake that was. She quit her job the next day and within weeks started doing drugs again. I tried to work with her to get her clean and sober again; it just wasn't meant to be. The final straw was one night when I was out playing pool and Mary, her daughter Diane, and Toni were at the house. I was supposed to be home at 12:00 midnight. Well, I was on a roll and winning and ended up running past the midnight hour; it was closer to 1:00 am. Instead of calling and getting yelled at, I decided to wait until I got home to get yelled at just once instead of twice. Man did I walk into a hell of a mess! Mary was waiting for me with my Samurai sword in her hands, threatening to kill me for not calling, coming home late, and for fucking around. She took a few swings at me, barely missing me before I grabbed the sword from her. I remember seeing my little girl Toni all curled up in a corner crying. I knew I had to do something and soon. This was when I decided to get a divorce and started mentally planning how to accomplish it. Luckily, Diane was there and called the cops. The first thing the cops did was handcuff me thinking I was the bad guy. Diane told the cops that it was her mom swinging the sword. They un-handcuffed me and asked if I wanted to press charges against Mary. I said no, I just wanted to leave. They asked if I had a place to go and I said yes, I would find a place. I went to my Compadre Cesar's house for the night.

The next day, I asked my Godson Tony for a vehicle to use. He brought over a clean, custom 1955 Ford Pickup to keep. This ride was for show only so I asked him for another vehicle and he said that was all he had at that time. So, I used it for a little while before selling it. I talked Mary into going back to rehab, which didn't take much talking. Little did I know that she had met a friend in there the last time around and that he was a drug dealer. Her parents and I visited her the first few days. Then I went in one day and they said she had checked out. I couldn't get a hold of her and she didn't contact me either. After a few weeks, her mom told me Mary met somebody in rehab and was living with him. At first, I was pissed that she would do this to Toni and me, and then I figured it was for the best. Mary moved into a hotel downtown called the Berry Hotel. It was a flophouse full of people down in their luck. Mary would call me from time to time to ask for some cash. I knew it was for drugs and would give her some sometimes; other times, I would say no and get yelled at. When we got divorced, I quit giving her money and just tried to bring Toni up the best I could.

A lady named Mary lived across the street from us, and we called her Grandma Mary. Grandma Mary had a son and grandson (John and Jonas) that lived next to her. Her grandson was a few years younger than Toni and went to the same school as Toni. So, Grandma Mary and I would eventually work out a deal that would suit both of us. I would bring Toni to Grandma Mary's house in the morning before I went to work (5:30 am), and she would take them to school. After work (2:30 pm), I would pick them up and bring them home. Plus, I would pay Grandma Mary $50 a month for snacks (I think I mentioned that in Toni's story).

1992, I got promoted at work to supervisor in the bindery.

After working the last few years as the lead mailing machine operator/ trainer, I was finally promoted to the supervisory level. I stayed on day shift and had the job of scheduling all three shifts for the daily and weekly job schedules. The job was easy yet very demanding. We had tight time frames for most jobs and had to complete them or be fined. I took to the supervisory job like a duck to water. It was easy because I knew the machines and the personnel's strengths and weaknesses. My biggest problem was with another supervisor (Godfry) and the State Manager (Gladys). Godfry was from the private sector and had no communication or personnel skills. He was very confrontational and a bully. Gladys, on the other hand, was a closet lesbian who hated a man with intelligence and authority, especially if he was under her. Gladys and I bumped heads on more than a few occasions. But they both had to recognize I had skills when it came to the equipment and the employees I supervised. I could get much more production out of them than they could ever do. The employees respected me for my knowledge of the equipment and the fact that I respected them as well. To this day, the production level has never been better than when I was a supervisor in the bindery. We went from producing, on average, 75,000 pieces of mail per mailing machine per shift to 124,000 pieces of mail per mailing machine per shift. I made sure the machines were maintained daily and weekly. I also made sure the operators were constantly being trained and updated on mailing codes and procedures to bring better cost savings to the customer. All the equipment I was in charge of had a desk manual or video to train new operators on the operations and maintenance of the equipment. I kept all the equipment supplies stocked and as high an operational mode as possible. I had a great relationship with my employees while constantly battling with Godfry or Gladys on their wants and needs.

1993, I started training Leroy.

Leroy was the first kid I officially trained as a boxer. Leroy was a young 12-year-old who had a father named Sam, a mother named Elaine, three sisters (Elizabeth, Jeannie, & Cloey), and a brother named Sammy. Leroy was the youngest in his family. They lived in Galt, California, had a very loving family, and would take turns bringing Leroy to the gym. I have to admit, his sisters, though younger than me, were very beautiful looking, had beautiful bodies, and above all were just good people. I didn't think too much about them romantically, I just enjoyed seeing them when they were around the gym or the fights; they had an energy about them that was undeniable. Eventually, I was brought into the family as if I were one of them. I would visit them in Galt or be invited to their birthday parties and graduations. Eventually, Sam and Elaine divorced; it got ugly then. Sam left her for a young Filipino woman and Elaine was not too happy. Leroy still fought and won a couple of titles, such as Golden Gloves, Diamond Belt, Silver Belt, plus was a finalist in the Junior Olympics. I had other fighters who were good, too, just none better than Leroy. I taught him everything I knew about boxing, and he used the skills to the best of his abilities. He was my proudest accomplishment as a boxing trainer.

1994, Dad had a stroke and I helped out at the gym.

First of all, I couldn't believe Dad had a stroke; he was in such great shape. Either way, I got the call while I was at work. I pulled up to the house as the ambulance was pulling away. I followed it to the hospital and quickly parked and joined Ma, Ellie, and Louise as we waited for the doctor to let us know how Dad was doing. By the time the doctor came out, my brothers Johnny and Nathaniel were there with a few friends. The doctor took us to a private room and told us dad would never be the same and he probably had less than a year to live. He would also need to go to therapy to learn how to talk, read, speak, and walk. We really couldn't believe what the doctor was saying to us so we just took turns coming to the hospital and visiting or assisting the nurses as best we could. I even brought his dog "Spits" to the hospital to visit (after the hospital agreed). It didn't take long before dad was using a three-legged cane and walking again. He had to learn how to talk and read also. Within a year, he was up and about doing what he liked even though he still had to use the three-legged cane.

1995, I was going full throttle working as a Supervisor, training kids at the gymnasium, and raising Toni.

I felt like a well-oiled machine, constantly moving and not slowing down for anything. Work at the Printing Plant was busy as it should be in the printing industry. The gymnasium had me busy during the week and off to matches every other weekend. Then there was Toni, my constant companion by my side every inch of the way. She is such a blessing, no problem, just a roll with the flow kind of kid, no complaints whatsoever.

I felt so blessed to have the strength to do all that I did and never get sick or complaints from anyone. All of that was out the door in 1996.

1996-1997, I got discriminated against at work for a job that was ruined and cost the state $1,400.

The thing about it all was that Godfry had really screwed up a job that cost the state over $120,000 and Gladys screamed and threw the product all over our conference room to demonstrate her displeasure with our handling of this specific job. The whole Printing Plant had to endure this fiasco and witness it, which worked out for me in my case against them. It was especially since I had gotten an "atta boy" earlier on the job I was working for being able to save it by reformatting it. Later, Gladys decided it was a bad idea and had my superintendent write me up for it going to the customer in a different format than originally planned. The customer did not complain, only Gladys.

Then, some of the women from my past started to join the bandwagon. They tried to file a sexual harassment suit against me that backfired. It all started when I first got promoted and I stopped seeing some of the women I dated as a Bookbinder IV. They didn't like that idea but I had to tell them I couldn't be with them because I was a supervisor. One weekend when I was supervising some of the women from the mass mail unit, they didn't show up for work. I had to write them up for failure to appear at a scheduled mandatory weekend work schedule. Three of them got together with some of the other women from the plant and decided to file a sexual harassment complaint against me for telling some of my sexual exploits to them. It was later regarded as retaliation because I wrote them up.

I was actually demoted back to Bindery worker IV and was not in the least bit worried about it because I knew they were in the wrong and I had the main body of the bindery on my side. I have to admit, I was a little worried because this was the state government and I was against these white folks who did not care about how dirty they wanted to get to rid me of my pride and respect. So, I went to work documenting my case with the help of many people from the plant who loved and respected me. By the time we had our first court appearance, my Equal Employment Opportunity (EEO) discrimination case was filed with the General Services EEO office, the Department of Fair Employment and Housing (DFEH) office, and the EEO Council (EEOC). My case against them was strong and the judge saw this when I went to court. She actually rose up her right hand and said (and I quote) "I see a big red flag in this case!" Then she proceeded to read off my personnel file and all the commendations I had over the years with no mention of wrongdoing except for the recent case. They wanted to demote me and did! She gave them one week to come up with a better case and for me to get a lawyer.

Even though I did all the right things leading up to the court case, I knew I had to hire a lawyer. I was lucky enough to find a great lawyer who had actually left the government lawyering business but took my case after reading it. So, within a week we were ready and in court again. Let me tell you something, the court couldn't have opened up with a better scenario. Here I was sitting with my lawyer and next to us were my superintendent and the assistant state manager and their lawyer. All of the sudden, the judge walked in and she and my lawyer act like they hadn't seen each other in years. They started to catch up on family and the past in front of all of us. Inside I was cracking up as I looked over and saw the sour look on those three faces. The judge then started to read both of our cases to herself and decided to ask us if we would like her to mediate the case, explaining what mediation was about. I agreed and they told the judge they had to get the OK from Gladys. So, the judge allowed them to call Gladys and she agreed on the mediation. We went back and forth on what I wanted and what they were willing to give up for me. I knew early on they still did not have a real case against me and I decided to go for the Associate Governmental Program Analyst (AGPA) position I wanted. At first, they wanted me to stay a supervisor and work in the Pressroom. I declined because I knew nothing about the presses. Plus, I felt they would have a better chance of demoting me and firing me as a press supervisor. They decided to offer another position in another department. Again, I declined their offer. I asked for an AGPA position in the plant along with not working with or around those individuals who discriminated against me. They agreed as long as I dropped the DFEH and EEOC cases. I did and thus, in 1996, began my future as an AGPA in charge of the State Administrative Manual (SAM) unit.

What I failed to mention about this whole ordeal was my true feelings. I felt I was being tested by someone or something. I had a terrible bout of depression, tried the pills the doctors gave me only to feel even worse. I prayed and felt God's strength and with Toni at my side as my anchor, I became a better person. I had never felt the pain of having so many people hate me. Luckily, there were more people voting for me than were against. They were the other blessings that kept me going, as if I were fighting for them as well. After the final gavel was brought down and I prevailed, the employees saw me as a hero for fighting the system and winning, knowing the system was trying so hard and playing dirty to beat me down and out. I also learned a lot about the system and how it works. I eventually went back to school and became a mediator for the State Personnel Board and the Victim Offender Mediation Program through the Juvenile court system. I then went to school to become an Equal Employment Opportunity (EEO) Counsel and an EEO Investigator for the State's General Services Department.

CHAPTER 7

1998-2004 (43-49 YEARS OLD)

INTRODUCTION

My Dad passed away and my relationship went with him. I took over the Gymnasium working 12 to 14 hour days and was still raising Toni. In my second marriage, we adopted Catherine and Louie, divorced in 1.5 years, I went back to college, and I took Salsa lessons.

My Dad

On December 9, 1998, my Dad passed away after his third stroke in four years.

Valentino was a very proud man. He stood 5'8" and weighed around 160 lbs.; Dad was a solidly built man. He left Utah before I was born and moved the kids and Mom to Richmond, California. A year after I was born, he divorced my Mom and never looked back, taking all five of us kids with him. When I was four years old, Dad brought us kids to Central Valley, California, just across the river from downtown Sacramena. Dad was driving trucks plus loading and unloading trucks on the docks for the Teamsters Union as a Lumper. He sure had a lot of drive! As long as I can remember, he always worked at least two jobs, sometimes three. He always made sure we had a roof over our heads, food to eat, and clean clothes. Dad was a firm yet fair parent most of the time. He didn't curse or drink much and was always in a good mood. He enjoyed a good joke when he could, loved boxing, and was into giving us kids whatever we needed. He made sure that when we turned seven years old, we were training (boxing); he wanted to make sure we could defend ourselves. Even Gina, the oldest and the only girl, knew how to box. I even saw her work over a girl in the neighborhood with that boxing; she sure looked good! When we first moved to Central, Dad had a broad named Vicky take care of us. Vicky had two boys, one was older than me and the other was younger. Vicky would treat our family like shit and send us outside to play (really just to get us out of the house) while her kids were fed and got to watch TV. She would do this when it was cold or hot outside. When we complained to Dad, he would not believe us until he came home early and saw it with his own eyes. He grabbed Vicky and threw her out along with her sons and their clothes. It was a happy and sad moment for us because now we had to see the look in Dad's eyes wondering how we were going to be taken care of. It didn't take too long until he brought home Eva and her three daughters named Lea, Bee, and Yoyo. Eva had two sons, too. Antonio was the younger of the two and Floyd was the oldest, both were older than the girls. They lived somewhere else but visited often. Eva was the greatest person I ever met! She was your typical Mexican lady; she always had something cooking on the stove, such as beans, soupa, tortillas, etc. Plus, she was always cleaning something, clothes, towels, floors, etc. Her daughters were always helping, too! They were older than me and mixed real nicely with our family. Dad eventually got Eva pregnant with our little brother Julio. Can you imagine living in a 3-bedroom house with four brothers and four sisters? I must say, it was cozy and we did get along real well. Eventually, Dad had to buy a station wagon to haul us kids around; luckily we didn't need seatbelts back in those days.

My Dad's Mom (Grandma Ruth) got sick when I was around seven years old or so. His sister Ester and her kids Anita, Ruby, and Vinnie moved into the house across the street from us so Dad could have them close by. Dad was actually buying that house for them to stay in and care for their family and ours. That's when he started working three jobs and sleeping when he could. I enjoyed having Grandma living across the street; she was on her death bed and still had enough energy to tell me stories about my Dad and his brother's adventures while growing up in Salt Lake City, Utah. Grandma Ruth eventually died and was sent to Utah for her burial. It's the last time the family took pictures together. After the funeral,

Aunt Ester and her kids stayed a little while longer then moved to East Los Angeles, I haven't seen them since. Dad must have loved to work because he just kept working and saving money. He always said, "If you want something bad enough, save for it and pay cash." He did that his whole life. He paid cash for most of the things we had, such as cars, furniture, appliances, etc. He even paid cash for the gym and the house that came with it. But he worked very hard for what he had and he took very good care of them, too!

When I started to box at age seven, I was very happy to do it, especially since hearing the stories my Grandma told me about the fights both on the streets and in the rings that my Dad and his brothers had. I wanted to be just like them and eventually did do just that.

My biological Mother Elaina would come by every other year to visit and show off her new husband (she had six or seven by the time she committed suicide or was murdered). Mom was so full of spunk; she could light up a room just by walking into it! She was full of energy and was very beautiful too! Mom took me to Colorado to stay with her, her husband, and their kids one summer (it was for a couple of weeks). I was probably around five or six years old, but I do remember being in the chicken coop with the husband's daughter. She was around my age and we were showing each other our parts (if you know what I mean). That was the first time I saw a cooter; it was small, bald, and very strange looking; kinda like something was missing. It was the first time I encountered chickens, too, specifically a mean and crazy Rooster. That fucker kept chasing me whenever I went by his house. When we came back to California, Mom asked my Dad if she could keep me. Dad asked me if that is what I wanted to do. He also said if I did go I would not be allowed back. I stayed with him.

I can remember the only time I ever saw my Dad cry. It was when he and Mom were talking and she left (which usually meant we would not see her for a few years). I didn't know what to do, so I just backed out of the room; he didn't see me. I guess Dad really did love Mom, and that was the last time any of us saw her alive.

I can't remember Dad being too personable with us kids. We did not see him much because of the work he did, but we knew he loved us and I, for one, was very proud of him and loved him very much too. I would have to guess that having such a big responsibility in raising two, sometimes three families and having to work so much would be a big strain on his body and mind. Dad sure didn't show it, though; he was very strong like that. When he was around, I do know that every night before we went to bed we would hug and kiss him good night. I still remember his scent.

The old Gillette Friday Night Fights were something we'll never forget. When they were on, the one thing you never did was get in front of the TV. If you did, you either got the boot or the belt. Dad was very serious about the fights and wanted to study and enjoy them as much as possible. Being kids, we made that mistake a few times and he was quick to snatch us up, work us over, and not miss a punch on TV. We would laugh (silently) when one of the brothers got caught. I actually enjoyed sitting there watching the fights with him. He would bob and weave, slip and punch along with the fighters. That's how you can tell former boxers when they watch fights on TV; they do that. That was also the only time he would relax and have a beer.

I got caught stealing some silver dollars from the neighbors one day and when Dad got home, he asked me where they were. I took him on a wild goose chase looking for them. We went for a walk around the neighborhood for about an hour before I finally remembered they were under my mattress. Dad was a good sport about it and I didn't get in big trouble with him; mainly because I stole the money to buy him a present for his birthday that was coming up. We talked about it, and I believe that is when I decided that talking about the crime or wrongdoing was better than a beating. I believe that is why I didn't spank my children; talking is much better.

When I was 10 years old, I broke into my elementary school with an older 14-year-old guy from the neighborhood. We broke about 27 windows, spray-painted shit about the teachers and the principle, tore up a few desks, and sat around eating cookies and drinking sodas in the teachers' lounge. When we went to get our bikes, the cops were waiting for us and took us to the police station. The dude I was with started crying like a big baby saying his mom was going to kick his ass and that he was in trouble. I tell you, I got pissed off! This was a big white boy 14 years old crying like a baby, and here I was a very small Latin kid, 10 years old, thinking what a pussy. I told him so, too! Plus I told him, what do you think my dad's going to do? Needless to say, he was off my Christmas list!

My dad had to pick me up at the police station, I felt bad for that, mainly because he was very disappointed in the destroyed items at the school. He/we had to pay for it. The courts made a deal with him/me. I would work it off at the school as a janitor. Later, I noticed the judge knew my dad from the fights at the Memorial Auditorium. Dad usually had fighters fighting or was a cornerman for fighters coming in from out of town. Judge Bonetta liked my dad and gave me a break by letting me work the damage off. I did such a good job that summer, they hired me as a part-time employee. The supervisor was a very kind person named Mrs. Campbell. She was an old, heavy-set woman who adored me. She would take me to her house at lunchtime to feed her mother and me. Mrs. Campbell even started me on a savings account with the Bank of America. I tell you, she was very nice and kind to me.

My Dad bought me a Schwinn Stingray Bicycle when I turned 11 years old. They were very expensive and were also the bike to have back then. I had that bike looking real good; Freddie and I were into Stingrays and kind of customized them before they were popular like now. We would have the long banana seat, with the long sissy bar, chrome fenders, white walled tires, custom paint job, two rearview mirrors, tassels hanging from the handle grips, and an extended front fork. My first one was stolen in front of the old Fox Theatre while I was inside watching a movie. When I got home, my dad made me walk back to Sacramena and report it to the police. By the time I got home it was very dark and cold. Dad bought me another one later that year and I let one of Gina's friends borrow it; she sold it, the bitch! Her name was Janie. She said it was stolen but I found out she sold it to someone in Gardenland. My next bike was my oldest brother Johnny's old newspaper delivery bike. It was a 24" chrome bike; it was a big bike that was real heavy duty, and I kept that one for a long time.

My next ride was a motorcycle. Dad helped me buy that one. It was a Honda 160 bored to a 205. We bought it off of Tino. His Mom (Isabella) was one of the ladies that took me in when I got caught stealing from her store. I loved riding that bike; I would take it out by the river and go up and down the hills and through the trees and bushes. The final ride was one warm summer day; I was going over these two hills that looked like humps. The center was a deep groove with about a 20-foot drop. I guess I wasn't going fast enough and didn't quite make it over the second hill and the bike and I dropped into the center 20 feet down. My nuts were slammed into the seat and the bike and I just lay there for over a half an hour in misery! When I did get enough strength to get up; I noticed that the back rim was bent crazy. It still ran, though, and I drove it home with the back tire wiggling back and forth all the while my nuts were still in pain. I sold the bike that weekend to Georgian for $100. He had that rim fixed in a couple of days and was riding it all happy. Georgian was a crackup; he was an albino, with big ears like a monkey, he stuttered, and would tap/stomp his feet when he was nervous trying to talk. He was a mess! But all and all, he was a nice guy. I saw him later in life and he had gotten his ears fixed and didn't have the stutter any more. He was actually a very successful business man.

OK, back to Dad…When we moved from Central to Sacramena (Tahoe Park), I started training real hard just because we had our own gym and it was fun. The rest of the boys did it because Dad made them, except for Nathaniel; he just liked beating people up, kinda like me too. When I turned 15, a guy named Richard (Rich) Kalob wanted to train me, and my dad asked me if it was ok. I said yes and that was the beginning of my licensed boxing career (it's in another chapter). Dad was my cutman/cornerman during my amateur and professional career (which was great!). Actually, Dad was the man the Boxing Promoters would hire when they had boxing matches in Sacramento and surrounding areas. He was one of the best cutmen/cornermen around. Dad used to give me these rubdowns the day before a bout, and I tell you! He would rub out a sore muscle and make you pay in the worst way. Dad would crack me up; he would be sweating, making faces, and rub out that sore like he was exorcising the demon out of you. It would hurt at first but afterwards you would feel like a slinky all relaxed and loose. The day of a fight he would make sure that everything was in order and that you as a fighter had nothing to worry about, everything was under control. Being around Dad during the fights was very rewarding to me; I felt very close to him during those events. I think that is another reason I wanted to box so much; making Dad happy and watching his reaction before and after a bout was priceless.

The rest of my brothers and Sister Gina argued with Dad a lot. I wasn't an arguer, it's like I said earlier, talking was much better. So, growing up, I would just let him holler at me and beat me if I did something wrong and not say much. I think that's where I got his respect. It would hurt to have him holler at me for no reason or should I say not a good reason but, I would stop listen and leave for the day or two. Usually when I got back he would have a present for me, I think it was his way of saying he was sorry. It was usually something that had to do with a motorcycle or a jeep (like a belt buckle or t-shirt). We had a good understanding of one another; it was beautiful.

When Dad retired from working at Safeway, loading and unloading trucks, he was close to 67 years old. They say the only way they could retire him was by closing the warehouse. I decided to buy a house close to him to make sure I was there for him if and when he needed me. I bought my house in 1989 and the house was just five blocks away. I would make sure and stop by a couple of times a week just to say hi and to check up on him.

Like I told you earlier, in 1994, Dad had a stroke (he was 72 years old). The doctor did not think he would live another year; we believed differently. His speech was gone, he couldn't walk or feed himself, and his mind was not all there. Dad went through a lot of rehabilitation during the next few years. He was very hardheaded as usual, which was a good thing. Before you knew it, he was talking so we could understand him, he was walking using a 3-legged cane, he was feeding himself, and he started to get his sense of humor back. During this time, I would go to his house and take him to get his hair cut or do little things around the house for him. My brother Nathaniel would do the same when he was clean (not on the Heroin). I took him for a ride to Folsom Dam just to go for a ride. That's when he told me that being in his condition was the shits. It was during this time that I took over the gym and was running it under Dad's supervision. Dad got better after a while, and then a few years later he had another mild heart attack. We were in the gym and he was sitting there with a few of the guys joking around and bull shitting. I was standing next to him when one of the guys asked me if Valentino was alright. He had a blank stare and was motionless. I knew he was on medication so I thought it was a reaction, so I had one of the kids (Leroy) go next door to the house and ask Tressa if he was supposed to be that way, she came running over and said no. We immediately called 911; luckily there was an ambulance a few blocks down. They were there in time to stabilize him and get him to the hospital. I'll never forget the look in Leroy's eyes when he looked at me and saw the look in my eyes.

That time, he was sent to a Sutter Hospital where we had a couple of second cousins from Dad's first cousin Anita there. They were supervisors in the trauma center for Dad, and they made sure he got the best care; he was their favorite uncle. One night, I showed up to find my dad was all strapped down. I asked what the hell was going on. The nurse told me Dad was very abusive to the nurses both verbally and physically. I told them that my Dad wasn't that kind of person, so I untied him. It was funny because when I did untie him I found a few razors underneath his arm that he was going to use to cut his way out. Later, my new Mom Tressa told me they needed to get him off the medication they had him on because it caused hallucinations and that was what was wrong with him. Once they changed his medication, he was back to normal and they loved him. Johnny was there that night crying on the floor like a baby; it made my Dad mad and he asked me to get him out of there because he was acting like a sissy. The next day, the nurses told me my brother was not allowed in the hospital with that woman because they caught them having sex in one of the spare rooms. What a mess that was. He denied it but still didn't bring her back.

We got Dad back home a few weeks later and he was doing ok. He was maybe better than he thought because one day, Tressa called to tell me Dad had taken off in his truck with Jake, Tressa's grandson. Dad wasn't supposed to drive because of the heart attacks, but did anyway. I was out looking all over for him; so was Ellie, Tressa's daughter. I asked Tressa if she had any idea where he could of gone. She said he was talking earlier about getting a haircut and that none of us (his sons) would take him. I found him at his Barber shop sitting there like nothing was wrong, shooting the shit, getting his hair cut while Jake was sitting there with a mouth full of candy and both hands full of more candy. When I walked in, he introduced me and acted like nothing was wrong. I let him know he wasn't supposed to be driving and he had Tressa and Ellie very worried. He got mad and told me he'd been asking us to take him to get his haircut and we wouldn't do it. I didn't argue, I did ask if I could take him back home, but he wouldn't allow it. He insisted on driving himself back home. Jake was telling me that people were yelling at him on the way to the barber shop because he was driving so slowly. I believed him because on the way home he did the same thing. The following day I took out the distributor cap so he couldn't drive anymore.

Dad's last heart attack was at home. It was on Dec. 9, 1998 one week after Tressa's birthday. I was at work when I got the call from Ellie and left and was at the house when the ambulance was pulling away. I followed it to the hospital, parked, and was in there when they were taking him out of the ambulance. It wasn't long until the doctor came out and escorted us to a private room to explain his death. The family will never be the same… We were able to visit his body one more time before they moved him to the mortuary. That was a mess; Johnny, Nathanial, and Ellie were crying out loud and grabbing at Dad. Mom, Rena, and I were silently watching when the doctor asked me if I could have them quietly leave because they were making too much noise and commotion.

The funeral was nice; we had a lot of family from the San Jose area here, along with those from Utah. Plus, a lot of boxing fans and friends were there to pay their last respects. Nathanial was up front talking about Dad to the crowd and saying stuff about Dad and him smoking pot and about some of the other things they did and he just kept on like it was a comedy show. Finally, the family was getting a little nervous about some of the stuff he was saying and we had to take him off the floor. Poor Yo-Yo was up there by herself and was crying and having a very hard time trying to say what she wanted, so I went up behind her and put my arm on her shoulder and let her know I was there for her and she would be alright. She finished her speech and was ok afterward. I didn't have anything to say, I'm really not a speech type of person. I was there for the rest of the family and friends who wanted to talk. I was dating Nichole at the time and she was perfect at the after-funeral reception at Mom's house. Nichole acted as a hostess and was feeding and cleaning up without even being asked. I will never forget her kindness and sincerity while we were grieving our loss. I was very serious and did not cry at or during any of this ordeal; I had to be strong for my Mom and family. It was after the funeral and after I pushed his body into the crematory furnace that I broke down in my sister Gina's arms. Dad will always be missed and never forgotten, I'm very proud of him for all he did for all of us and how he did it, mostly by example.

At 42 and as a single parent, I was running a boxing gym with Rudy. I eventually inherited the California Boxing Gym. It was a slow process of getting with the other trainers in the gym and eventually with my Marine Corps buddy Rudy, but we turned the gym around. It had 12 volunteer trainers (both amateur and professional). It ran from 8:00 am until 8:00 pm.

We had four different boxing clubs training out of the California Boxing Gym:

1. Brian Boxing Club with Brian and Brandon as the owners and trainers.
2. Adam Ants Boxing Club with Fred and Diego
3. Mayhem Boxing Club with Barrack.
4. The California Boxing Gym with Rudy, Markam, and yours truly.

Running a Gymnasium was made easy by the people involved. The other clubs would pay set monthly dues. I would collect from my members and add that to the total take for the month. It wasn't much but it did the trick. I would get one-third, Mom would get one-third, and the last third would go back into the gymnasium for bills and equipment. We would also fix or repair whatever broke in the gymnasium, and if it cost them anything, I would pay them back. Most of the time they would not accept my money, but I did offer it to them in honesty. There were many different characters in the gymnasium that made it so much more enjoyable to be around. It was also universal in its nationalities. The early club would be a nice mix of Latinos and Blacks, the afternoon would be mostly Blacks, our club time would be a mix of all including many women, and the last would be mostly Latin and women.

We would sometimes have a potluck boxing match between the clubs for fun and entertainment. There would be no winners, just match them up from the different clubs and more or less spar, eat, drink, listen to music, and have a lot of fun. The different families from all the different clubs would bring food, drinks, and music. We would pack the house with family and friends. The event would last most of the day.

The same went when we had events to attend such as the annual Golden Gloves, Diamond Belts, Silver Gloves and the many other types of competitions. We would help each other get fighters ready for battle by supplying sparring partners or vehicles and money for the trip. Whatever a fighter needed, we supplied. We wanted to make sure they kept focused on the fight and that we had their back. I remember buying some of the kids their boxing shoes, headgears, mouth pieces, whatever they needed to fight we supplied.

You see movies about fighters and the gymnasiums they come from and they all have the same atmosphere. You have the good fighters and the not-so-good fighters all in the mix. You have the fighter who is a role model and the one who is not. You also have the people who frequent the gymnasiums, such as the local hoodlums, the promoters, and the want-to-be managers. But, no matter what or who is in there, the place is home to many. I remember when we closed the gymnasium and had a closing party at Luigi's Pizza Parlor across the street from the Gymnasium. Some of the guys were visibly upset and a few were teary eyed. I still see some of the people who used to visit, train, or pass by the gymnasium, and they all have great things to say about it. They say they remember how hot it was in there in the summer and watching the kids jumping rope in front of the gym, and how they would see them run around the block. Plus, they mentioned how good the water was and that we should bottle it. It was really good especially in the springtime when it was very cold.

I can only remember two times when I had to get physical with someone in the gym. Once there was a guy who came in all drugged up and was talking shit and wanted to get into the ring and fight/box someone. I invited him outside (I grabbed him by the collar, dragging him outside) and said if he wanted to fight it would have to be outside the gym unless he was a member, he left. Another time was when a well know fighter from back in the day came in and was getting all belligerent with me; I socked him in his chest and knocked him down. I proceeded to drag his sorry ass out of the gym, too. Oh! there was another time but I believe I told that one in the Cesar part, when he came in and wanted to fight knowing if he ever hit his wife I would be looking for him to kick his ass for putting his hands on her. So, he came in wanting to fight out on the streets, I had him wait hoping he would change his mind (he was my friend you know). He didn't, so we went outside and a couple of the kids were sneaking a peek from around the corner of the gym and witnessed me letting him take a few shots at me before I slammed him against the wall of the gym and dropped him with an up close and personal shot to the lip. The kids got a kick out of it and he felt better. I didn't, though. He was a friend and my Compadre; he just shouldn't put his hands on Evelyn.

I would have to say the thing I miss about the Gymnasium the most is the constant bullshit we would pass out with each other. We were always talking shit to each other and never let it get out of hand. We also made sure the kids who trained in the gymnasium kept up with their homework and respected their parents. One kid who trained with us for a few months was probably around 14 years old. His mom would bring him in and sit and watch from the seating area. The kid would yell at his Mom to bring him some water, or to get him his mouthpiece or to tie his handwraps. He even had the audacity to call her names, which was the bottom line for me. I sat him down and in my most convincing voice let him know that if he ever talked to his Mom like that again, I would kick his ass. Then I explained to him the significance of a Mother and how disrespectful he was to her. I continued to let him know how hurtful it was to her even though he might not see it. I noticed she didn't say anything to us as I was dragging his ass to the backroom either. I did get my point across and loved seeing the respect he was giving her as they were in my house. When they had to move because of her job, I remember them coming to the gymnasium to say goodbye. She told me thank you for the talk with him and that he got that way from seeing his father talk to her that way, which was why they divorced. She also mentioned he was doing better in school as well. He, on the other, hand didn't say much. He just gave me a big hug and a Marine Corps statue of the Bull Dog and the USMC Emblem along with a thank you. I also have a picture from one of the younger kids on my desk at home. It is of a drawn picture of me and the kid at the gymnasium and the kid is mentioning that the gloves are too big and in the background a sign that reads "We can train anyone. Well maybe?" It is very nicely detailed. I also received a "911" commemorative statue of two firefighters and a policeman next to the American Flag. The compliments I do appreciate are the ones about my father. I get them from guys and girls who were kids and training under his watch. They are all grown up now and just to hear them and to see the look in their eyes makes me feel great! I make sure I tell Mom about them as well; she enjoys hearing about Dad and his past students. The gymnasium had rules such as no sagging pants, no cursing, no spitting on the floor or ring, no hanging on the ropes of the ring, and no jumping on the ropes in the ring. There were more, I just don't remember. Oh yeah! No rap music when I was there and respect each other.

The Gymnasium has beautiful paintings on the outside that were never vandalized, and for an area like ours, that was an accomplishment. There have been a lot of Champions who worked out at the CBG, including Pepino Cueves, Bobby Chacon, George Foreman, Sugar Ray Leonard, and a few local Champions such as Tony and Sal Lopez, Pete Ranzany, Richard and Mario Savala, Benny "Shotgun" Garcia, to name a few, a very few. Along with the many characters, the CBG will never be matched in any way, shape, or form.

1999-2004

It was June 9, 1999 (6-9-99) and I was in love with Elizabeth.

Elizabeth was 31 years old and I was 44. I had known Elizabeth as Phil's wife, Joe and Ali's mom, and Leroy's older sister since I started training Leroy. Our daughters were a few months different in age and used to attend pre-school together at David Lubin Elementary. I would see Elizabeth at the after-school parent/teacher meetings in the classroom. We would be there to learn how to communicate and play with our children, under the guidance of the teacher. At the time, Elizabeth was a short-haired Lesbian and divorced from Phil. Later, when they remarried, I would visit them when there was a birthday party or something special happening. Elizabeth and I kind of liked each other's company, and would just talk innocently in the beginning. I would see her at the Blockbuster video store and other places in the neighborhood and we would just be cordial.

Then, Leroy joined the Marines and we (Leroy's family and I) made the trip to Old San Diego for Leroy's graduation. Elizabeth drove her family there and I drove Sam and his girlfriend. Elizabeth and I were racing all the way there, passing each other up and trying to outdo one another. Man, were both of our cars full of mad people when we finally got to San Diego. We didn't care. As a matter of fact, I was excited by the race and I felt Elizabeth was just as excited. I started to have a strange feeling about her and she felt the same way. Even though Phil was there with us, we didn't care and just flirted back and forth. I was falling in love for the first time in 20 something years. I didn't care that she was married, I didn't care that we were surrounded by her family, I just knew I wanted her in my life now and forever. I could feel her energy very strongly when she was in the computer room of the hotel. Elizabeth was typing something for her job on the computer and I was standing behind her, it seemed like I was on a cloud, first of all, just for being alone in the same room with her and because I could feel her energy and inhale her scent. It didn't help that earlier we were in Old San Diego and had a few large Margaritas with our dinner, and Elizabeth's Old Man Phil got a bit angry with her for it, too! This went on even when we left the Marine Corps parade deck and Leroy's graduation, when I told Elizabeth *"I miss you already..."* just before we hit the long ride back to Sacramento. Luckily, Elizabeth and I were still in charge of the driving and decided to stop at the shipyard and have lunch before the drive back. We were able to flirt and take pictures again. The ride back was just a fun as the first, fast and furious!

Elizabeth and I secretly kept in touch over the phone and eventually met at Miller Park on June 9, 1999. That was when we first kissed and fell in love. We had to see each other when we could after that. We even have a song that I sang to her when we were sitting in the back of my Jeep Wrangler making out and just talking, "Always and Forever." To this day, I get flashbacks of the song and our circumstances surrounding it. Whenever we felt the need to talk with each other, we could and would meet at Miller's Park, just to talk.

This is an example of how hot I was for Elizabeth. Our first sexual encounter was at my 10th Avenue home, and Elizabeth barely made it into the entryway when I started kissing her beautiful red lips and went down on her sweet shaved pussy. It was small, tight, and very delicious. Little did I know, she was on the rag. Man was I horny for her, she finally got a hold of my business and I'll be dammed if she did not take the whole thing into her mouth and throat. That was the best cock sucking I've ever had. I believe our second encounter was at her home on 2nd Avenue. I knocked on the door and Elizabeth opened it and inside candles were lit and the place looked very neat. We didn't make it past the first couch we hit, full penetration, I could feel it going all the way in and to this day I get hard just thinking about it, especially since it was the house she was sharing with her husband. Maybe I'm a thrill seeker or something, it could just be that I am in love and blind by it all. One of the most memorable moments was when we met at Tahoe Park and the most amazing thing happened while we were hugging. It was a warm evening, darkness had already set in when we had just kissed, and not just a kiss, we were very passionate with our love and it felt as if it would be our last kiss every time. While we were hugging, a strange feeling came through us, it was as though a spiritual being had just passed through us. We both (still hugging) looked at each other and asked, did you feel that? We both said yes and from then on, we knew we were connected by greater powers than ours. I still can't believe what had happened, but either way, I knew I had to have her as my lady for life.

It was only a few months later that she moved in with my daughter and me on 10th Avenue. She brought her son Joe (15 years old) and daughter Ali (11 years old). Let me explain Joe and Ali. Joe was from Elizabeth's first husband, she left him when he got abusive and little Joe was only a few years old. Phil, Elizabeth's second and third husband adopted Joe and gave Joe his last name. Ali was Elizabeth and Phil's daughter. Ali is a beautiful young gifted girl, very personable, yet could be hard to get along with at times. Joe was a spoiled kid, more of a momma's boy. It was a struggle trying to keep peace in the family at first. After a while, it got better, but only by a little bit. Elizabeth was very good at organizing things. For example, Elizabeth organized a Fourth of July Block party for 10th Avenue. She was able to get most of the neighbors to help get a jumper, face painting, apple bobbing, basketball games, water balloons, squirt guns, plenty of food, and later that night, over an hour's worth of fireworks. That evening, we all pitched in and cleaned up, too. That event was the best Fourth of July party I ever attended, and I owe it all to Elizabeth.

After living with each other for a little over eight months, Elizabeth started disappearing and not answering her phone or returning calls. I noticed a change in her appearance, such as her hair style and color, the clothes were different, her nails, and makeup. I sensed she was cheating on me and I started to get paranoid. This was woman I fell so hard in love with that I just couldn't see living without her. Then her attitude was just plain mean. After trying to talk to her for weeks and trying to communicate my feelings, I got frustrated and kicked her out of my house on a cold November night in 2000. Elizabeth immediately bought a house two miles from our home and changed jobs and just tried to move on like our love had no meaning at all. I, on the other hand was devastated and suicidal. As I was looking at our pictures, I noticed the changes in her appearance and how she had changed. She still wouldn't talk to me, so I started talking with her family and showing them the pictures. Her family told me that was what she had been doing for the last 14 plus years to Phil and her children. I finally had a chance to talk to her and convince her that she needed to see a doctor.

We went to a few different doctors and they all agreed Elizabeth was bipolar. We start reading different books on bipolar disorder and its effect on people and families. We even went to a couple of bipolar counseling groups along with her son Joe. We decided to fight this disease and moved back together, minus Joe – he stayed in Elizabeth's house on 58th Avenue. Elizabeth had to experiment with a few different drugs in order to find the right fit. It was very hard on her and I sympathized with her. I know her mind and body were going through hell! But, we were able to get through it and stabilize her mind and body. We were connecting more and more each day.

Elizabeth and I had a pact. We would have a weekend a month alone; it was our time to bond and unwind from the house and family, and it was a time to get crazy with each other and have fun. Elizabeth booked a trip to the Berry Patch; it was a small cottage by Point Reyes. The couple that owned the place were older hippies. The old dude named Jerry (he looked like Jerry Garcia) would stutter and hop on one foot to the other, kind of like a rabbit. It was hilarious, especially since he had this long scraggly salt and pepper hair, wore baggy clothes, and actually looked like an old hippy. When he saw my California Boxing Gym Tee-shirt and I told him I used to box as an amateur and professional, he about went unglued and said No Fucking Way! He proceeded to hop and stutter like nobody's business. Next thing we knew, he told us to wait and ran into the house, bringing back an old 1921 boxing Book from the University of Los Angeles on how to box. It was the most colorful boxing book I ever read. To this day, I still get it out just to reminisce about him and our time at the Berry Patch. And since I'm reminiscing, Elizabeth and I were loaded (on weed) and you know how I get on weed! Elizabeth had her back to me facing the kitchen window; next thing I knew I was feeling her up and down and getting some from behind, damn she had a sweet looking ass!

All was going well. We visited the Point Reyes Lighthouse and just strolled down the many steps to the Lighthouse. The view was gorgeous, the wind was blowing, and we could see for miles. I felt very close to Elizabeth as if we were one with the universe. On the way back up the many steps, Elizabeth stopped to lean on the hand rail and strike a pose as if she was tired. Her long dark curly hair lying on her shoulder was very beautiful. I hope I still have the picture. There was an Indian Reservation nearby that was having a powwow. Elizabeth and I visited the Reservation and sorta participated in the singing and took in the energy filling the land. It was a wonderful day to be alive.

My 47th Birthday at the Torch Club

It was one of the best birthdays I ever had! Elizabeth looked so beautiful in her black dress; she started out by renting a limo to take us to a fine dining establishment. Then as we went from the restaurant to the Torch Club, the chauffeur poured us a drink to celebrate the occasion. Once in the club, we were escorted to our reserved table by the dance floor. My sister Ellie, my brother Johnny, my daughter Emma, Niece Angel, and a few other close friends partied with us. We danced and drank until we could not see straight. We left a mess! Luckily, we still had the chauffer. I don't want to get into the specifics of the rest of the evening but my Elizabeth sure knew how to treat me.

Our next trip was to Napa and the Great Wine Train Dinner and Calistoga's local Anderson's Health Spa. Again, Elizabeth planned this Wine Train Dinner and weekend. Let me tell you about this so-called dinner! We got all dressed up to go on a train ride at three to six miles per hour for approximately three miles one way, then back. We got fed a little something every 15 minutes. I was hungry and kept trying to get them to give me my meal all at once or stop long enough for me to run to the Burger King down the tracks and across the street. All in all, Elizabeth and I were just cracking up and having a good time. I really don't know if it was as soon as we got there or before we went on the Wine Train Ride that I proposed to Elizabeth. I was so much in love with her and losing her earlier proved it to me in so many ways. My God, I loved this woman with all my heart, mind, body, and soul. The next day we decided to rent a Harley and just ride. Luckily the guy that rented the bikes liked us and didn't charge us full price and said if we came in after hours it would be no problem, just knock on the back door. I don't know if it was Elizabeth's first ride on a Harley, but she did enjoy it as much as I did. We went around the town and into the surrounding hills. Everything was good, life was wonderful.

We got married in the Rose Garden at McKinley Park in Sacramena. It was one of the first times Elizabeth was on time! My Elizabeth was the most beautiful woman I had ever seen in a wedding dress! The picture I have of her waiting with her flowers in her hand, made my heart melt every time I looked at it. We went to Lake Tahoe's Lakeland Village resort for our honeymoon. The wood cabin was just gorgeous; it had a nice old fashion feel to it with a large yard, strawberries, and other fruit trees. When we went horseback riding by the lake, the day was just beautiful. It seemed everything was the way it should be in life. The bicycle ride through the back woods and town was excellent, the clean air and the brisk ride felt good, and we were laughing and having a good time everywhere we went.

My life was never better, I was never happier either. We adopted a 10-year-old girl about to get taken from her mother who was a drug addict. Her father died three years earlier in a work-related accident. Katherine (10 years old) was her name; her older sister Louise used to train at the CBG and they lived around the corner from us. The next thing you knew, we adopted another kid, this time a boy whose parents were drug addicts. Louie lived with his uncle who was physically and mentally abusive. Louie was 16 years old and a skate boarder. He started out to be very respectable, and then went to smoking weed and stealing. We had to buy a bigger house in order to keep the family together, so we moved to La Riviera and Folsom Blvd., just a half a mile from the American River, into a five-bedroom home with three bathrooms and a pool.

Somewhere in between all of this (I really can't remember when), Elizabeth got a boob job. I liked what she had but she wanted them bigger and rounder. It was fun looking at all the pictures and getting to pick which pair we liked. When they were healed and ready for the world, they came out beautiful! I believe her attitude (confidence) changed a little too, not that it needed more of it.

New Year's eve 2002, we went to Sausalito California; it's at the end of the Golden Gate Bridge. We were staying at the Casa Madrona Hotel overlooking the Bay, Golden Gate Bridge, Alcatraz Island, and beyond. It was a rainy day, so we shopped, ate, drank, and walked around all day, besides the stop in the room for a little nap and boom-boom. That evening, we went to the Club Margarita for some more food, drinks, and dancing. There was a group of Puerto Ricans that came from (I believe) San Jose via a charter bus that made the evening more enjoyable by selecting the music and just being very entertaining all evening. When we left the place, we walked (staggered) toward our hotel along with a lot of other couples, actually saying Merry Christmas instead of Happy New Year. Oops! That's how much fun we were having. Everyone out there was happy at 1:00 a.m. 2003.

Elizabeth's depression set in a few months later. I found out she had been taking her mother's pain killers along with her medication for the bipolar. Next thing I knew, she was depressed and had my gun. Her sister Cloey called me to tell me the news. Cloey was at our house with the kids (who were all frightened). They told me she walked out of the house with the gun in her hand. I don't know how I figured she would be at the park (Tahoe Park) but she was. I was able to approach her and talk to her. My poor baby was very depressed and there was nothing I could do to stop it. So, I just stayed there and sat with her, and we talked. That was when we decided to have her admitted to a suicide prevention facility. I already knew she was doing the downers and let the facility know. They did the test and confirmed it. We (the kids and I) visited her every day for the three weeks she was in there. She gained 40 something pounds by being on the anti-depressants. I could tell she was not happy with herself, but I didn't care what she looked like, she was the love of my life and my wife. I was going to stay by her side no matter what.

So, during that time we went to Collin's Lake for a family camping weekend. Again, we had so much fun; Jeannie, Leroy, Cloey, and our families were all there. We hiked along the lake and beyond, into the other side of the dam where there was a very cold stream. We (the kids and I) took turns jumping into it; damn it was cold. My favorite hiker was always Jessie; she was the one who always fell behind and whined about being too tired to go any further or her feet hurt. I was usually the one who had to carry her (she was so heavy, solid heavy, that is). We played stickball, went fishing, rented a boat (and actually let the kids take turns driving the boat), swam, and just plain relaxed. One night we were playing Dominos, Ali, me, Joe, Louie, and Toni. We were talking so much shit to Ali, she got so mad at us and started crying and was mad the rest of the night (I told you she had attitude). I liked the hikes to the little store (approximately 1 mile), where they had the best ice cream cones. Again, Jessie had to stop and get carried after whining about her feet hurting or being tired. She was so cute when she was mad.

Then we had the pool party for, I believe it was for, Leon at our house. What a mess, there were so many kids and parents there you could walk across the pool on top of their heads and not touch the water but what fun. We were throwing the kids in the pool, playing basketball out front, BBQ'ing, BS'n, all day.

It wasn't long after that Elizabeth lost control again. I had my undefeated female Golden Glove fighter (Vickie) staying with us for a little while since she had nowhere to go. She just got back from the bay area where she tried to start a new life. Things didn't go too well and she was back in town (for the record, she's a lesbian). Around the same time, Elizabeth started leaving the house early and showing up late at night, not wanting to come upstairs and sleep with me. I would go downstairs and find her watching TV with the kids and Vickie or on the computer with Vickie (later, I realized Elizabeth was in the same close position I was in with her when we were in Old San Diego) or asleep in front of the TV. During the day, if she was home, she would make herself something to eat and not clean up behind herself and then leave again not talking to me or starting an argument before she left. It was getting close to Christmas time (November) when I noticed her coming home at night with Vickie, making excuses to go out of her way to pick Vickie up from all over town.

I could see it happening again, my Elizabeth was morphing again! She started dressing a lot more risqué, changing her hairstyle and color, nails, attitude, and makeup. I sensed she was cheating on me, and I start to get paranoid!

Christmas came as a very disappointing event. It was supposed to be a Christmas I was going to make very special to all the new members of our combined family; it ended up the worst. There was a lot of tension in the house. I was snapping at everyone. I felt weak and beat down, at the same time broken hearted and defeated. Then it happened. I lost it when she finally would not listen and fell asleep downstairs again. I woke her up yelling at her to come to bed. When I went upstairs to go to bed she followed me and started yelling at me while I was lying down. I jumped up, grabbed her and threw her on the bed. It was there and then I knew she was not the Elizabeth I loved and she had to go before I threw her through the upstairs window. On December 30, 2003, she was gone.

At 48, I was broken hearted. Elizabeth moved back to her house, and Vickie left, too. I still saw Vickie at the Boxing Gym and we would hug and be cordial. Louie kept in touch with both of them. Elizabeth and I tried to keep in touch and stay friends. We actually still slept together a few times and were sort of trying to decide what to do. I found out six months later she had been sleeping with Vickie and Louie knew about it all the time! I started asking questions and found out that everyone (my daughter's Emma, Katherine, and Toni, my Mom and Louie) knew about them being together. My kids saw them lying on each other downstairs. Louie would be with them after school partying with them and other things. That was when I lost it! Luckily Louie was not home, so I called Elizabeth and asked her about it. She denied it all. I finally got it out of her and I completely lost it! I threatened her life and Vickie's too! For a week, I looked for them, knowing if I saw them, I would go through anybody that got in my way to kill them! If I was driving, I would have run over anybody to get to them! I had completely lost my mind! I joined the 24-hour gym where Vickie worked out just to ask questions and find her. I went to the Starbucks where she hung out to tell them to tell her I said hello. I was actually driving by Elizabeth's Mom's house looking to hurt Elizabeth. After five days of looking, I decided to stop and just let it go. By then it was too late; Elizabeth had a restraining order on me. I lost my wife, my adopted son, a dear friend, and my wife's family. I was suicidal, homicidal, and at a loss for words. I was barely getting to work or eating. I still had a gym to run and two daughters to care for.

2004, I was 49 years old and felt it. Wow! I couldn't believe what just happened. I quit the boxing business in February, closed the gym in March, and sold it in November. I started reading a lot of different spiritual books trying to find myself again, including going to college again, and writing poems, short stories, and My Perfect Woman…which is a description of the love of my life, Elizabeth.

MY PERFECT WOMAN…

I was told to Remember: Whatever happens, happens for a reason, I was told: Don't try so hard, the best things come when you least expect them. I was asked to write down my perfect woman; to write what she looked like, what she felt like, what she smelled like, what she tasted like, what she sounded like, and most of all, how she made me feel inside (spiritually).

It didn't take me long to figure that one out, since most of my life I have known what I wanted and usually got it. But what I didn't get was the sound or the spiritual connection, what I didn't get was it on paper. My thoughts about the perfect woman were never clearer than they are today and will be for the rest of my life. I will not wait for things to happen; I will not expect them to happen either. I will hold on to my true heart's wants and needs til my last breath or until I find this love that I am so deserving of. I have been faithful and honorable to a lot of people in my life and now it is time to do the same for me…

My Perfect Woman… has dark hair; straight, curly, or wavy, it didn't matter. Breast wise, it didn't matter as long as she had nipples big enough to caress and a nice bottom to really caress and look at. Her skin had to be soft to the touch and clear clean bronze-colored.

My Perfect Woman… has eyes that are dark yet gentle, the sort of eyes that could see right through you, all the way to your soul. Her eyes would talk to me, I could read what she wanted just by the look in her eyes. Her eyes would look at me with love, respect, honor, and pride. Her eyes would tell me every day how safe and loved she felt with me.

My Perfect Woman… has lips that are round and soft, with a natural red that made you want to kiss them every time you passed them. The kind of lips that lured you to them from the other room, just because they were there… you would probably call them magnetic… Out of those lips came the words of truth and love for each other and all those that were ours to love, our families and children…

My Perfect Woman… her hands would be soft, yet strong. Fingernails short, yet feminine. She has hands that want to touch and feel me ever so close to her all the time... Her hands are like miracles, if I have an ache or pain, all she has to do is touch it and it will feel better. She knows how to touch and feel me when I need and where I need it the most, Everyday...

My Perfect Woman... has hips that would naturally dance when she walked, with a waist that would be very small and firm to the touch. Together, they would talk to me when she walked into or out of a room. And when naked, I couldn't hold myself back, not for an hour, not for a minute...

My Perfect Woman... has legs that are very athletic; they would have to be to hold up such beauty and poise. The legs would be firm and soft to the touch and taste, with feet that are small and delicate...

My Perfect Woman... physically, above all, would have a smile that would light up my heart every time she smiled at me. The smile would make me feel wanted, loved, and secure...

My Perfect Woman... would feel physically firm, yet soft to the touch. When we made love, she would make me feel like my whole world was surrounded by her, we would be as one in our connection, (our spiritual connection). She would look at me and have me feel the love coming from her heart, a feeling only a spiritual love can send. That feeling could only come from her, to me. Equal to the kind of love a mother has for her only child, you'll know that this is the one that you are connected to unconditionally for the rest of your life...

My Perfect Woman... did not have a specific smell to her, she had a scent, a scent that would capture my heart and make it skip a beat every time I was close enough to her to smell her... I would want to hug her and take in all that she had to give me from that scent and her heart to mine. Her breath would be clean and natural like the air we breathe, always inviting me in closer to kiss and caress her body and soul. I would know and feel this scent for the rest of my natural life...

My Perfect Woman... would taste sweet, soft, and would keep me hungry for more and more... Her kisses fresh as the spring water we drink, her neck and body soft and sweet, with a gentle nudge to keep me coming back for more. When I gave her oral sex, we would connect as one and I would know exactly where to touch and feel at just the right moment.

My Perfect Woman... would have a voice that was gentle and soft like that of a newborn baby cooing... She could talk to me and make everything bad, good. Her voice would tell me all the things a man wants to hear that are good, pure, and loving. I would hear her voice and my whole body would stop, just *to make sure I didn't miss a word, for I know that she is telling me something that is from her heart... Her voice would never speak down to me and would always be true, no lies, and straight from the heart and soul...*

My Perfect Woman... has and always will have a spiritual connection to me, even in the afterlife. My body trembles and my heart races when I anticipate seeing her or knowing that she will be close to me. I get anxious waiting for her to come home, to be next to me. When I watch her get out of the shower and get dressed and put her make-up on, I feel connected to an angel, my personal angel... When we hug and kiss we feel so safe and calm; I can only imagine the heavens feeling this way. When I have her close to me, I can smell her, taste her, and hear her giving me energy and I can feel me giving her my energy. We are feeding each other our everlasting energy for life and love. I could kiss her hand and feel the love emulating from within.

We are connected as one body, mind, and soul, and as one heart with a love that will conquer all...

By now you might think, what planet is he on? I am in a world of my own, a world where I make things happen for my child and me. A world where I don't get hurt by love... I am not going to stop believing in love and the spiritual connection I once had. If I had it once, and it is true that there is a spiritual connect to someone out there, I will look again, since the first one was not the real one, only a tease, of what really is supposed to be true, honorable, respectable and real...

I will fight the temptations from the wrong women and begin my Journey as a Warrior, hunting, gathering, plotting, and believing there is a person such as the above that will be my soul mate forever...Paulo 9/24/04

When I look back at the times we had (both good and bad), waking up and going to bed each night with a kiss and an *"I Love You,"* I realized I was fighting for a person I could not win. Being a loner most of my life, Elizabeth filled me with love like I never had before, plus her family gave me a feeling of a real family. Elizabeth and I had a saying etched into our wedding rings that I thought would hold true always and forever, *"Love Conquers All."* I guess love does conquer all. I have had a hard time since then to let love into my heart, or love someone else. My Love for Elizabeth has conquered me...

I now know I cannot turn back the hands of time and decide to sell both homes (one I owned on 10th Avenue and our home on Clearlake Way).

I sent Katherine to live with her sister Louise, and Toni and I moved to 14th Avenue in Sacramena. It was a beautiful Spanish-style home that sat on ¼ acre of beautifully landscaped land. The house had 2½ bedrooms, a fireplace, custom interior walls and ceilings, a Jacuzzi tub, it was just beautiful. Plus it had a small studio in back for guests. The only drawback is that it had no garage. Eventually, I had Joe (my step-son) build a carport big enough for a trailer and a vehicle. Joe did a very good job with the help of Javier, his future brother-in-law. I also added a 10'x10' Tuff-shed for the motorcycle, my tools, and cleaning stuff.

2004 at age 49, I decided to go back to Sacramena City College to study Motorcycle Mechanics.

I knew of a couple of people attending the classes. After talking to them, I decided to enroll. The initial class was an overview of the other classes that covered the motor, frame, transmission, and electrical. Right out of the gate, the class was unorganized! The class was overbooked and we were stuck taking the class in the auditorium. The books we had to purchase were not in stock. Then when we did purchase them, the instructor told us they were obsolete and that we would just need one of the three books purchased. To add more bullshit to the class, the instructor told us to all sit together up front in the middle rows so he could see us and we could hear him. This pissed off half of us since it was the middle of winter and some of the students had colds and flus. Then on top of that, the class consisted of a few young students in their early 20s and more students in their 30s to 40s. The instructor talked about his past experiences and did some nostalgic storytelling. Most of us were more pissed at him for talking bullshit rather than getting on with the class. The class was scheduled for 2½ hours, but most of that time was spent hearing the instructor's crap! I saw many students quitting every week. Then there came the test! We were instructed to go by what the instructor said and not by the book. Therefore, if we didn't listen and take very good notes we could fail. A lot of students failed the first test, me included. I decided to stick it out and try harder. After the second test and another failed attempt, I decided to quit the class before it stayed on my permanent record. By this time, over two-thirds of the class quit, most of them just walked out, but not before yelling at the instructor for being an idiot (I was one of them). The frustration got to us pretty good.

2004-2005 at age 49-50, I decided to take Salsa lessons at the Ballroom Dance Studio on Folsom Boulevard.

The first three months were the most frustrating. I was told in the beginning that it would be very hard to learn in the first few months, but that I should keep coming back until I got it. They were right! I ended up taking private lessons with Leann that helped a lot. I eventually started buying DVDs from Salsa San Francisco and that was the turning point in my Salsa Dancing. That is also where I met Angel Eyes, Toni's future Godmother and my very dear friend. Angel Eyes would come over once a week between the Ballroom lessons and we would practice the salsa, have a few drinks, and sometimes have dinner. We became pretty good dance partners and went out a few times to dance and have fun. Angel Eyes truly was a blessing to Toni and me. We kept in touch for a few years afterwards, then just lost touch...

CHAPTER 8

2005-2011 (50-56 YEARS OLD)

INTRODUCTION

By 2005 and through the first three years of living on 14th Avenue, I cut down an ugly-assed Palm tree, an even messier Black Walnut tree, a dying Oak tree, a weird-assed tree that dropped a lot of shit all over the place, and three very thorny lemon trees. I planted two Redwood trees I brought back from the Redwoods in the back yard, four white birch trees (two in the back and two in the front), three different types of palm trees in the front yard, two big ferns for the front porch area, and a nice weeping willow for the front yard. Every year I grow various tomato plants and keep my 16 different roses looking good. I even have a nice variety of colored jasmine plants all over the front yard. They all keep the brick wall with white wrought iron fencing and light fixtures surrounding the front yard looking very elegant. Oh! I even planted a beautiful blue colored plant/flower that my godchild Rissa gave me for my 52nd birthday in the center of the brick planter in the front yard.

I went back to school and took a poem-writing, short story, and biography class. I wanted to get a feel for my biography and some tips for the writing style. We were to write a short story about whatever we wanted to. One of the young female students' writing was off the wall. She started talking about a friend who liked to give blow jobs and how she would get off by doing these blow jobs. The author kept saying she was really concerned for her friend because she would just be talking to guys and out of nowhere start discussing blow jobs, eventually saying how good she was at it until the guy would take her up on it. Kind of like a hook and bait tactic to blow guys. But, the funny thing was that she kept saying "her friend," while we in the class kept thinking that she was actually the person she was writing about since she was so explicit about how to blow a guy and how it felt to do it. Since we were in a writing class and couldn't really laugh or make rude comments about her story, after the class was over, a few of us were discussing her story and all of us came up with the same answer, she was the person! After that class, she was never seen again. I really enjoyed the class and got a "B+." I also got to write a lot of good stuff to get some issues off my chest. I enrolled in a Spanish class that was very interesting. The teacher was speaking in broken Spanish most of the time, which was kind of good. The students were the most fun to be around. It was very hard to understand the class subject since it had to cover some stuff I hadn't used in over 35 years such as grammar, syllables, pronunciation, etc. Then we had two books, a DVD, and the Internet to use to do our homework. I tell you, I was very confused but passed, eventually receiving a "C" in the class.

January 8, 2005 I started to build the bike of my dreams...

I started to build the custom motorcycle of my military dreams. By that, I mean, I can remember drawing out a custom motorcycle like the old Rat Fink models with the big back tire and long frame and oversized motor. The bike would be called a Paladin as in "Have Hog Will Travel." The Paladin means Heroic Champion or Trusted Defender of a Noble Cause. The only bad thing is that around late 1990-2000, other builders were making bikes similar to what I had in mind. One of the first I saw was a Ground Pounder. The only difference was that the Ground Pounder had a rigid frame. So I had a little catching up to do. First I went to Molly's Custom on Del Paso Blvd. in North Sacramento. After six months, I realized it was going to be an uphill battle. The people I started with (Molly) were rude and non-professional. The cost was going way over budget and I was not getting what I paid for. The next thing I knew, I was $30,000 into this bike and had nothing to show for it but a bunch of parts, many that did not even fit the bike. I went to another builder at Sac City

Choppers. The owner informed me he was the President of the Sacramento Chapter of the Devil's Own and asked if I had a problem with that.

I said I did not and that he had great recommendations from mutual friends. So I went to Boss, the President of the Sacramena Chapter of the Devil's Own, with my parts and 2½ years later I was still not riding and in a bigger mess than before, over $53,000 in the hole. It's not like its Boss's fault, it's just that the original shop I went to did not order the correct parts for the type of bike I had envisioned. If it was not one thing it was another, such as parts not fitting, the wrong wiring harness for the fuel injection, battery not strong enough because the bike frame would not fit the bike motor, the tank inner sealant not holding and needing a new sealant job which called for the outer and inner paint to be removed, then the starter not strong enough, and the starter gears being the wrong size. I'm telling you, this bike was a nightmare. I did learn I had to be very patient with it or else I would take it out on my daughter, which I didn't want to do, even though I did catch myself getting angry at her for stuff that was not entirely her fault. I just let things get out of control with the bike; I was sitting on a very expensive bike that just wouldn't start and that I couldn't trust to get around that block on. Finally, on June 9, 2009, the bike (Paladin) was running great and looking good too! It has a G-Carburetor and is painted a Paladin's Black Cherry (I named it myself since it is a custom paint job). It has a red undercoat that looks dark red when it is in the sun it and looks Pearl Black when in the shade. My first time out, I took it to a bike show at the Dixie County Fair. I didn't want to park it across the street from the fair so I drove it in and entered it in the Bike competition and won second place. I didn't even wipe it off or anything.

Time to cover some of my past friends…

The Curse and the Prayer

When my daughter was young and impressionable, I didn't date a lot of women. As my daughter got older, I started to get back to my old ways and put myself out there.

Little One, Mary, Angel, Sally, Ethel, Nichole, Elizabeth, Rachael, and Angel Eyes were all women who were married when I met them and got divorced while I was dating them. Two of them I married, the rest were women I would party with, have sex with, then eventually I would leave them for another or in the end, just out of respect. One part of my curse was with the ones I married; they both got on drugs and left me for another person. That left me with the other part of the curse, which was being alone never to have a long-lasting relationship or a happy, forever lasting marriage. You have to realize these women were in bad marriages, the kind who were going nowhere and getting worst as the years went by. I would talk and listen to these women and hear and feel their pain as they told me the horror stories of abuse; physical, mental, and sexually tormented abuse. All of them had children who had to live through it all. Some of them were too young to know what was going on in their parents' lives and blamed me for the breakups. Some of the others loved having me around for the security and happy person I was and how I would treat them like my own children.

There are also the women who were and still are married and whom I've slept with who actually seduced me. I had been with these women for many years; they have grown children and are actually grandmothers. They are Carrie and Estelle, and they are both the same size and are very horny! Their husbands are much older than them; so when they come to visit, they don't waste too much time with the introductions. We make out, get naked, and have foreplay (usually they come during the foreplay) then we get down and dirty. Then we kiss and say goodbye. It's a very good arraignment for us.

Little One

Li'l One and I worked at the Printing Plant. Li'l One was a Bookbinder II running the lower end bindery machines or feeding pockets on the larger machines. I was a Permanent Intermittent employee. She would sit with us guys at break or during lunch and listen to all our dating and partying stories. I guess mine were more interesting than some of the others, so she started to talk to me and soon she was confessing her need to be out of her marriage and get a new man in her life. Li'l One was 4' 11" and built like a brick shit house. I mean she had big round boobs, and a tight round bubble butt and beautiful long brown hair. She definitely could fill out a pair of jeans and a t-shirt. She also had big, beautiful blue eyes. She wasn't happy with her husband for being a drunk and rowdy redneck, so we started going out to pool tournaments (Li'l One was a very good pool player). The sex for us was always a wild ride; she was such a screamer! That body of hers kept me going most of the night; she was very tight down there (if you know what I mean). She had two daughters who just loved me, and I loved them back. We never moved in, just stayed at each other's house and enjoyed each other's company. We were together for a couple of years until she got too far out on drugs and started tweaking; I left her for Mary.

Mary, my first wife

Mary and I worked at a parent company of The Printing Plant called Support Services. Mary worked as an Executive Secretary. Mary was a 5'4" blond haired beauty, very thin on top, but very nice and round on the bottom. She had a beautiful smile, nice full nipples, a tight cooter, and was always fresh smelling and very clean. She was just the opposite of Li'l One when it came to personalities. Li'l One was loud and very outgoing, kinda like one of the guys. Mary, on the other hand, was soft spoken, very quiet, and reserved. She also had two daughters; one loved me, the other didn't. We had a smooth transaction into our relationship; she moved into my house in a matter of months, got divorced and we were happy. We partied a little at first then she/we started partying with her cousin Lynn, her boyfriend Wolfgang, and Lynn's friends (Devil's Own and the Lone Ones). We'd hit the local biker bars and before you knew it, we were at home fucking until the sun came up. We definitely liked the sex a lot! Eventually the partying caught up with Mary and she started to become a tweaker and we had an on-and-off relationship for a couple years. It meant she would move in and out of my place. Eventually, we split and she moved to the bay area to a place called San Carlos. In 1989, there was the big earthquake in the bay area that prompted Mary to want to move back to Sacramento. I agreed to let her move in with me until she found a place of her own. Before you knew it, her cousin Lynn was pregnant and dropped off a little baby girl named Toni. Mary and I married, adopted Toni, and seem to be living the happily ever after dream. Mary started getting on the drugs again and went in and out of rehab, eventually hooking up with one of the drug dealers in rehab and moving in with him. We divorced and she married the drug dealer and I kept Toni. It was during the rough patch with Mary that I knew it wouldn't last and I started eyeing other women and met Angel.

Angel (My Puerto Rican Girlfriend)

Angel's dad (Bro) and I worked at the Printing Plant. Bro worked in the Pressroom where I started working, and then eventually I worked in the Bindery. I met Angel one evening after Mary attacked me with my Samurai Sword and the cops intervened and I walked out of the house borrowing my God-son Tony's Custom 1956 Ford pick-up. I saw Angel sitting at the end of the Bar called The Pit having a few drinks with a couple of her friends and one of her sisters. I asked her (or she asked me) if I could take her for a ride. I said and she said yes and that was the beginning of a great friendship.

Angel had these big boobs with the biggest nipples I had ever seen and a very cute smile to go with her outgoing personality; she stood 5' even, had short nappy hair, and was dark skinned. I eventually started affectionately calling her my "Puerto Rican Girlfriend." Again, I heard all the stories of abuse and as usual she came on to me and I didn't turn her down. We ended up playing softball together, going hiking together, and partying as well. Angel worked for a Law Office. Angel had three girls; they all hated me, blaming me for their parents breaking up. Angel stayed in her home in the North area while I stayed in mine in Tahoe Park. We'd been together off and on for over 16 years, and as of 6 August, 2007 I was still seeing her. She was the one I really enjoyed the most because she asked no questions and let me be me, plus she treated me like a king! Everywhere we went in the vehicle she would just start to blow me; it didn't matter, day or night! I loved the way she loved to please me! When we had sex, she was very easy to please and made sure I knew it too! My Angel was very fun in and out of the sack. Eventually, I met Sally and we became long-time acquaintances.

Sally

Sally was a tall 5'9" beauty (even more so when she wore those high heels!). She had long, thick, brown hair; a beautiful smile; was light complexioned; and knew how to wear a short dress to accentuate those long legs and make those hips sway. Sally was one of those girls you could treat like one of the boys but looked like a model when she dressed up. She had a habit of picking all the wrong guys; the one she was married to when we first started dating was a scrawny looser. We did the party thing for a while since she worked in the Bindery office as a receptionist and I was a Bookbinder III running the mailing operations. Sally was my own sex toy. All I had to do was show up at her place and we would go straight to the back bedroom and she would suck my cock, I would eat her sweet tasty pussy, and then she would ride me until we both came. We had the perfect relationship. After a while we sort of went our separate ways still staying friends, even to this day we will go out for a drink once in a while. Sally had a daughter that just adored me and I really loved her; she was a good kid. Let's see…I think Sally has been married four times since we first met. In the middle of this mix was Ethel.

Ethel

Ethel had the cutest smile to her small round face. She had medium length brown hair and a nice round booty to go with her small waist and small boobs. Her husband was a complete redneck. He was a drunk, physically abusive, and had a terrible temper to go with his ugly mug. I don't understand how these beautiful women ended up with such a bunch of mean ugly men! Ethel stood around 5'5" and had a very nice attitude; she worked as our Bindery secretary at State Printing. She would argue or fight (physically) with her husband and then call me and come over to spend the night. I really liked her… I don't know how it happened but, she eventually divorced her husband and ended up with my drinking, fishing, and hunting buddy Lyle. They were a very violent couple in the beginning. Both liked to drink, do drugs (speed), and have wild passionate sex. Plus, they both had terrible tempers. They eventually settled down, got married and had a child together. By the way, Lyle was married and had three children while he was with Ethel; they divorced before Ethel got pregnant. Lyle quit the drugs and drinking but eventually died in 2002 of a heart attack while in bed watching TV, with Ethel by his side.

I had to take a break from women and concentrate on raising my little girl, so for two years that is what I did until I met Nichole.

Nichole

Nichole worked in the bindery mail section. Nichole was so much different than all the other women I seduced. Her beauty was both inside and out. She was 5'2," a little heavier than the others; she was a pure Mexican, with green eyes and an olive complexion. Her hair was cut short, brown colored, and curly. She even spoke broken English with a Spanish flair. We would/could go anywhere and have a blast laughing and joking around. She made me very happy when we were together! My daughter Toni loved her and Nichole loved her back even more. Nichole had told me of her husband's exploits with other women and how he would leave her every other year for another woman, only to come back without any explanation. So, when she divorced him, he was in shock and went all nutty, pleading with her and her family. He sabotaged her vehicle so she would call him to fix it. There was a lot more to it than what I am telling you now (maybe I'll come back to it later). Nichole's two kids were in their late teens; the daughter was signed up and training at the California Boxing gym with Nichole while we were first dating. The daughter and I got along great until she found out her mother and I were dating. I never did meet her son; I did hear he thought I was ghetto when he saw me in my Jeep Wrangler waiting for Nichole to come outside. I dated Nichole for two years until I finally stopped trying to get her to move in with me or have us get our own place. Her kids were the ones that kept us from furthering our relationship. It was during the last few months I was with Nichole that I started talking to Elizabeth.

Elizabeth

Elizabeth was my second wife and is in a chapter all her own. I don't want to repeat myself and will move on to Rachael.

Rachael

Rachael was a short 5' beautiful Philipina, with medium length brown hair and a dark complexion. Rachael worked in the Forms Unit of the Printing Plant. She certainly had dancer's legs; she knew how to dance all kids of styles and practiced martial arts too! Her husband was a jerk to her and the family. I never met her sons but they were the sunshine of her life and very athletic just like her. We just dated for a while until one night she sort of spent the night and we did the deed while she was on the rag, it got everywhere! Rachael had the second biggest, roundest nipples I ever had and a wet pussy to go with them! As for the rest of her, she was built (as we guys at work called it) like a boy, straight up and down. But those legs were definitely a big turn on to me! She was very sweet to me and we could talk and joke around all the time. She got a little depressed at times after her divorce. We only did the deed that one time and kind of stayed good friends afterward. I liked her a lot as a friend and we still talk once in a while. She's actually the only one who would admit she left her husband for me. That is what got me to thinking about all the other women. Rachael was not happy with her job at the Printing Plant and left for another position in another department. We try and meet once in a while to dance and party with friends but no hanky panky.

Angel Eyes

I was introduced to Angel Eyes through Chili. Chili told Angel Eyes I was from Central and I was taking Salsa lessons at the Ballroom Dance Studio. Angel Eyes met me there and we just took the lessons together. Angel Eyes was 5'4" with light brown skin and a very nice complexion. She had medium length brown hair with a medium built and a very pretty smile. Her personality is very closed at first and then she opens up just enough to know a little more about her. It took a while for her to loosen up and talk to me. She finally told me she was in a marriage that was not so good since her youngest son died 10 years earlier while roller blading at the young age of 14. I told her I had a daughter who was 14 and about my relationship situation.

I finally introduced her to Toni and they hit it off real well. Angel

Eyes and I dated for a while until her oldest son's friends saw Angel Eyes, Toni, Toni's friend Brianna, and me eating Pizza and playing pool. Angel Eyes had to tell her son and husband about us and they soon divorced. Angel Eyes is the kindest person you would meet once you got past her quiet demeanor. Toni and Angel Eyes are as close as mother and daughter as you can get, I think because Angel Eyes came into our lives when Toni was starting to hit puberty. I asked Angel Eyes if she would assist Toni in her female stuff and, eventually when Toni turned 16 years old, Angel Eyes found Toni a gynecologist and was with her through that transaction. I think they needed each other more than they realized. Angel Eyes and I had the sex and stuff only for a little while; I never got the chance to fully express myself with her sexually. She seemed to not be into the oral sex I liked to give or letting me suck on her nice titties. Plus, she took a long time to get off, while I was very easily pleased with her. I guess we weren't sexually compatible and decided to just be very good friends. We still go out of town and sleep in the same bed; we just don't have the sex. I usually have Angel Eyes over once a week for dinner, drinks, a little Salsa dancing, or a movie. We have become very comfortable with each other and realized Toni needs both of us.

The online dating game for a 50-something-year-old man...

OK, I'm on the hunt for Ms. Right for me via a website...

It's horrible! First of all, most women will look at me and see a young 40 something, clean, proud, happy, solidly built man and want a piece of me until they find out I'm 50 something years old. One actually dropped her jaw and after dinner never called back, (she was 42 years old!). Before that time, we actually met a few times and had great conversations! Others were a little more discreet; they just didn't push the relationship and eventually we became friends. These were the ones in their early to late 30s. I decided to quit dating 20- and 30-year-olds and stick with the 40- and 50-year-old women. I still get a lot of hits from the younger ones but now I tell them before we get started that they are too young and if they were older, I would have loved to be with them. Now they get pissy and say it doesn't matter, "I'm still a woman" and what not! I just laugh it off and walk away. The bad thing about dating women up to my age is that they don't take care of themselves like they should. They look old for their age, their bodies are not in very good shape, or they try to act younger than they are! So I quit the online dating game.

The two ladies I'm dating are beautiful, short, heavyset, fun to be around, and very horny! One has big titties and the other has the big bootie. They treat me like a king and don't ask questions. Even though I'm still looking for the perfect woman, I have to have my needs taken care of and for some reason I don't feel too guilty about dating these women. I know I should but I don't. Maybe because they know deep down inside I cannot commit and we are just making each other happy for whatever time we have, no questions asked. They know as well as I, that I do love them deeply; I just can't seem to say it.

A couple of other women I met in-between...

There's a Bar called the Kiss Me Club on Broadway in Sacramena that was a dive. I was sitting in there one night just planning on having a few and I was done. Then I looked in the mirror behind the bar and noticed an older woman walking in with motorcycle gear on, long blonde hair, and real big tits! I see she was sizing up the bar and its patrons. She saw me and started to walk toward me. I slowly turned around in my bar stool as she approached and we look at each other at the same time and she said hello.

I told her hi and we began a conversation about bikes. She asked me if I knew how to ride. I told her, "yes." She asked if I would give her a ride home on her Hog if she had one too many drinks. I asked to see her Hog, and she said, "yes." We took a walk outside and I saw she had a Harley Sportster. I told her that was not a Hog; it was a girly bike. She informed me she was a girl and she had two real full-dress Hogs at home. I asked where home was and she told me it was around the corner. I asked her if I took her home, how was I going to get back here. She said, "You're a grown man, you'll figure it out." I agreed and we headed back to the bar for a few drinks. We had a good time drinking and talking with each other and a few other patrons when she told me she had enough and wanted to go home. It had been a while since I rode a Sportster so I got on it and moved it around a little between my legs to weigh it out. I asked her to put the helmet on and said she needed to hold on. Her bike was brand new and sounded good for a Sportster. She directed me around the corner and only five blocks from the bar. When we pulled up to her place, she hit the garage door opener and, low and behold, there were the other two hogs she mentioned earlier. Her place was a nice brick house right off of Southland Park Drive. It was kind of cold outside and when we got into her house she asked if I would like some homemade chicken soup. I said that would be nice. She served me up some soup and French bread and told me she would be right back and that she would make herself comfortable. While I was eating the delicious soup, she left and came back with a long see-through robe on with her big titties and nipples poking out. She asked me if I would like to strip down and enjoy her company. Of course, I said, "Yes!"

As I was sitting on the couch she dropped her robe and I couldn't believe her big titties. Then I got the shock of my life. As I was eyeballing her titties and started to stroll down her body, I noticed all the wrinkles! Wrinkles on her belly, her elbows, her knees, I mean her whole body was one big bag except for her titties. It's just like those comics where the old lady with the boob job is naked and these titties are big and plump and the rest of her is wrinkled and saggy. It was too late; she had me in a spot where I couldn't get away. Besides, my dick was already hard and I figured I better just concentrate on her boobs and not look anywhere else. Those tits were rock hard, not like the rest of her. She straddled my lap and was on me screaming and scratching and cursing. Even though she was a bag of bones, she was fun and tight too. She got her nut and I got mine, then I went to the bathroom to wash up. I asked her to warm up my unfinished soup. I went back in and she was trying to look her sexiest for me and I kind of smiled at her thinking about her body, then her tits. I finished up the soup and headed toward the door when she pulled me back in and gave me a kiss and her business card and asked me to keep in touch, saying it would be worth my time. I told her OK and headed back to the bar on foot. I hit the end of the block and jumped a wall behind the old Tower Records parking lot and walked the three blocks back to the bar. I got in there and the patrons we were drinking with earlier were just looking at me and smiling. I just shook my head and smiled back at them, ordered a drink and relaxed and enjoyed the memories of the past hour.

Another one that was big and delicious was from the Gymnasium. She had such a big butt that when she was on top I had to lean way to her side just to rub the back side of it. And, if somebody were to come in on us with her on top, you would only see my skinny legs dangling from under her. What I liked about her was her youth, solid size, scent, and laughter. She was a lot of fun, until she started getting boring; that's when I moved on.

Women and their needs...

As you have read from the beginning of Chapter 2, I've been having sex with women since I was eight years old and found out a few things I believe I should pass on about them.

Some women like IT to be called Love Making or Making Love, while others like IT to be called Sex, IT, or Booty-call. Not many call it Fucking anymore, unless you get caught with another women, then you're Fucking that Bitch! and so on and so forth.

Some women like to be cuddled during the day but not at night under the sheets, most do.

Some women love to be kissed and adored, some love the kissing some don't like the adored part (too feminine).

Some women like to have rough sex, some like it slow and easy.

Some women like to be massaged, some like to be rubbed down.

Some women like to be man-handled and cursed at during sex; some don't like the cursing but love the man-handling.

Some women will call me Joseph, others will have other names for me, such as Poppy, Pops, JoJo, Baby, Daddy, Honey, Sweetie, Joe Boxer, my King, etc.

Some women love to buy gifts for their man, others would rather cook a meal for them, some do both.

Some women are hot blooded for sex; others have to work for their climax.

Some women come quicker than me; others take a little longer. Most of the times we come together; either way, it's all good.

Some women like to drink or smoke pot before sex, others don't, most like to drink only.

Some women are aggressive toward me, others are timid; I like both.

Some women like taller men, some don't, most are good with my height.

Some women are loud during sex; others are quiet, while others are moaners. I love them all!

Some women are scratchers, while others are tight squeezers, again, I love both.

Some women love to suck dick, others (not very many) don't.

Some women love to swallow cum, others don't; most do swallow.

Some women can and will take the whole dick in their mouth, others can't.

Some women like IT on top, others don't. I love both including the side-mount and from behind.

Some women like role playing, others (not very many) don't.

Some women like blindfolds and handcuffs, others don't; count me in!

Some women like a light spanking, others like it hard. But they do like the spanking.

Some women are soft skinned and have a natural scent; some are not soft skinned but have a nice scent.

Some women love to ride on the back of a Harley, others don't.

Some women want kids, some don't. Most have them are grandparents at my age.

Some women like dogs or cats, some like other animals too.

Some women have great personalities, others are beautiful inside.

Some women are fun to be around; others are fun to have around (eye candy).

Some women like to have long hair, others prefer the shorter haircut. I prefer the long hair.

Some women like to have their hair pulled during sex, some don't. I'll pull hair in a New York minute!

All women want to be respected; some don't deserve it but get it anyway.

What I'm getting at is that all women are different in their needs, wants, shapes, sizes, and personalities. What I have found out about myself is that I love them all.

Below is a list of wants that I am looking for in a woman.

- I need and want a woman I can talk to and have fun in or out of the house with.
- Someone that can make me laugh.
- Someone I want to take with me around my family and friends.
- A person who is OK with my scheduled or not so scheduled naps and business.
- A person who does not mind my drinking and pot smoking once in a while.
- A person who does not mind me going off by myself for a few days if need be.
- A person who does not argue with me and is willing to talk over our differences.
- A person who has a good family, one I would be proud to be around.
- A person who is not the jealous type.
- A person I can trust no matter what the circumstances are.
- A person who can make me happy in or out of bed and whom I can make happy
- And last but not least, I would love someone around whom I feel comfortable praying.

Because if there's one thing I do know, it is that my life is in God's hands. If I am to have a woman, then God will provide her, if for a moment, a reason, a season, or whatever lesson I need. Both bad and good, and mostly good comes from these many relationships I've had. I've had to learn and have learned something from all of them. I have been hurt by and I've hurt the ones I've loved. But it does not get me depressed or feel unwanted because I know that when God knows I am ready, he will have a woman for me. If not, then I will please the women he sends to me until I am no longer able to. I hope I die before that time comes...

2006, Where am I???

I believe everything happens for a reason; yet, I cannot find that reason for why I am in such a hardship with my finances and relationships with women. Even though I have a nice home that is a financial disaster, a beautiful motorcycle I've dreamed of and have built that is another financial disaster, and women who love and adore me, I cannot find the one of my dreams and past prayers.

I've tried writing a list of my past and the way I've treated people and to try and make amends, but most of it had to be about the married women I've dated and I've come to grips with that. The rest of the things are really on a short list. I've noticed that a lot of bad has happened to me from people at work and in my personal life. Don't get me wrong, I am grateful for my blessings, yet they seem to come with a very big price in the end. A few examples are: I work hard and was promoted to Supervisor back in the 1990s at the State Printing and I treated everyone fairly. The next thing I knew, a group of women I dated earlier in my wild times who worked at Printing Plant started to file charges against me for various reasons and they got more women to do the same. Yea, I won the battle but lost the war. I ended up an Associate Governmental Program Analyst (AGPA) and moved into the Administrative aspect of the business where I'm still at today. But to go through all the Bullshit to get here, then do all the work I do, just to be told I am not wanted as a Manager last year was just too much!

Then, I worked and adopted children, got married to a fine young woman only to be cheated on and kicked in the guts by a dear friend I brought into our home; I'm left with my heart broken and wondering "why me" again.

I took over the gym when my Dad got ill and I helped out as much as I could. Then when he passed, I became the owner and my brothers told everyone they owned the gym and I ran it for them. Then the gym and mom's house started to fall apart. When we did have to sell her house, it was for far less than it was worth. And again my brothers got mad at me for selling and not giving them a fair share according to their way of thinking, even though they (mostly the oldest Johnny) did not do a positive thing with the gym or help me keep it going when it was open. They never

141

cleaned it, trained customers in there, helped fix or repair the building, or filled in for me if I was sick.

The home of my dreams is a cash cow and it's getting way too expensive to stay in every month because of a bad refinance I did. In 2004, I paid $302,000 with $30,000 down (I owed $272,000). After four years and two refinances, I owe $339,000 and am adding $1,000 every month because of the last bad refinance. Because of the bad housing market in the US, the house is not even close to what it was worth when I first bought it. I did a lot of upgrades that are nice, yet I'm still in the hole.

The Paladin Bike is completed and entered into the Easy Rider Motorcycle Show. The bike was cleaned, shined, and looking good for the show. I entered it in the special construction competition and walked away with nothing. I was under the impression that the bike would do great but the show was about who you knew, not how you did. I did not feel too bad; I was by the bike every now and then to listen to the crowd talk about the bikes in the show and how they liked mine. That was good enough for me.

I found myself at 51 years old wanting to learn a little more about God, specifically his way of life for us mortals/sinners. I received two Bibles when I went through my divorce, one from the State Printer Harry and the other from my dear friend Lupe. I have one at work and the other on my bedside at home. I've been reading about God and I am amazed at how vengeful he is if you are against him or his people who believe and worship him. I've tried to communicate with God through prayer to better myself and to get guidance. I feel at this time in my life he is ignoring me and is mad because of my past. I'm frustrated by God's ability to treat people the way he does just because he can. Reading the Bible is becoming a hardship in the sense that it is very disturbing to read his power and ability to destroy hundreds of thousands of people and his inability to save people in this date and time from the world in which we live.

2007 through 2008

So here I am damned near 54 years old and finally accepting and identifying the facts; I will never be happily married for the rest of my life, will never have biological children, will never have a beautiful long-term relationship, and I will have to live with the guilt of breaking up more than my share of marriages just to please my own ego. Knowing this has made my life a little more livable because before I was praying and wishing for a woman that would be mine forever and a day only to come up short every time. You really don't know how depressing and sad I would get trying to make sense of my love life. I gotta tell you, I do feel better knowing I have this curse rather than going on as if I will find a person to marry and have a child with and live happily ever after. This I have accepted and will live with.

So, after figuring what I did wrong to get God mad at me and wondering how could I get on his good side, I got to writing a prayer that suited my personal lifestyle and tried to do good wherever I went and in whatever I did and just trying to live a spiritual life. My faith was on the brink of destruction. I started to wonder what would happen if I went back to my bad self and just didn't give a damn about the consequences. Or, what is it I needed to do on top of all the things I'd tried? I started to get angry and I got careless about people and things, like I just didn't care anymore. The women I saw were of no consequence to me, the material objects meant nothing to me either. If it weren't for Toni I would have just moved from my place and got a little apartment downtown and lived like an old man should. I would have just gone to work and hung around the neighborhood, something I was doing but without the big monthly price tag. Toni knew a little about our financial situation but not all of it. I was pretty sure she would move with me when the time came and I would love it too. I just had to do it...I really was not thinking too straight with all of these hardships hitting me every time I looked around. It seemed I just couldn't get a break, even though I might have looked like I was a happy man and that I had a good lifestyle. I was really just living a very slow death and sometimes just couldn't see the light.

CHAPTER 9

2012-2018 (57-63 YEARS OLD)

2012

I bought a 2006 Road King Custom. I still have the Custom StreetPro motorcycle I designed and built I just take turns riding each.

Since getting out of the Marine Corps I've not been to open about being a Marine since I was never in a war. Which is good considering as of 2015 and 240 years since the signing of the Declaration of Independence there's been only 17 years of peace and I happen to be a Marine during 3 years of that time. Well Kitten I were at a Gun show and there were a couple of Marines at a booth selling Marine stuff just eyeballing me like I was fresh meat. One of the fellas followed us around for a few then finally stepped up and asked if I was a Marine, I said yes. He proceeded to tell me about the Marine Corps League and how they are committed to helping Marines past and present and their families, and if I wanted to join then as a member. I took his card and went to their meeting that Thursday, next thing you know my Lady and I joined the local Marine Corps League. We have monthly meeting, attend fund raisers, march in parades, and shoot in rifle and gun competitions. All for Marines in need and their families. It is very rewarding for us both since her Step Dad is a retired Marine and I was a Sargent in the Marine Corps. I was promoted to Sgt.-At-Arms after the second meeting.

The Printing Plant got even harder to go to in the mornings since I was being harassed by the Fat Assed Receptionist Laquisha, she thought she was running the Plant and would come and go leaving her reception area with no one to greet customers. Laquisha had a loud voice and would talk getto when her friends would visit and talk all nice when management would come by. I had to ask her to keep her voice down on more than one occasion. Others in our area would not say anything knowing that she would get mad or start crying and complain to management that they were harassing her. She started to harass me after I stopped her from walking a tamale salesman through the plant. She was disrupting the production area and the break times and management did nothing about it because she would always pull out the black race card or get mean with them and they would back down. She started staring at me with mean looks, making noises when she would see me and eventually would cut me off or block my path when we were walking towards each other in the hall ways. I complained to her manager, the state printer, the Equal Opportunity Office (which was the Workplace Violence Prevention Manager) and put them all on notice, that I was about to go off on her if she keeps this up.

On November 2012 was the final straw when I was approached in my office by the State Police. He told me that the receptionist had said that I bumped into her almost knocking her down in the hallway. I was almost speechless. I asked him to hold on for a minute while I opened up my documentation that I had on her harassing me for the past two years. He read the six pages and said that this sounds like an inside job for the upper management and that he could do nothing about what she claims and that I should see a lawyer. I also asked him if he talked to her. She's twice my size, how could I budge her.

It was immediately after that that I contacted my manager, the State Printer, and let them know that I was leaving on stress and that I would be filing against the state for all the years I've been harassed by her and the management for not protecting my rights.

2013

To make a long painful story short, after seeing my physician, my doctor-appointed psychologist, a state-appointed psychologist, and the State Compensation Insurance Foundation (SCIF) representative for the previous few months, I was awarded a nice lump sum and given back my vacation and sick leave time for being off on stress. SCIF actually made a few visits and phone calls before awarding me.

In March, I retired after 32 years with the Printing Plant. Retirement is nice and smooth at this time. I get up during the week at 0500 to make coffee for Kitten and me, we talk, and while she's getting ready for work, I make her lunch. Then I see her off.

Work at the MMA Fitness Gymnasium was picking up with the fighters. I was also doing a lot of personals and putting on Cornerman's classes on the different legal professional handwraping, and cutman classes. The first five months I was able to travel to Utah and Tokyo, Japan with the fighters. My favorite was Tokyo with its clean streets, tall buildings, no road rage, and soft-spoken people. I loved the experience visiting there as a civilian rather than as a Marine.

I forgot to mention, I sold motorcycle parts for my friend Arman from Arman's Garage. Arman lived next to me and he bought Harleys and other motorcycles and sold them. He ended up with a lot of extra parts and I sold them for him and got half the profits. It was a nice arrangement for the two of us since I had the space in my garage for the stuff plus the time and he did not and we both made extra cash on the side. I called my part of the business CycleParts916.

So between my retirement, the MMA Fitness Gymnasium, my personals, and CycleParts916, I had a nice paycheck each month. Life is wonderful each and every morning knowing I have God in my life and that I have no worries. I'm living comfortably, and do not stress on anything. I've been helping out my nephew and trying to keep my daughter Toni in college.

Kitten and I have also joined the Patriot Guard Riders (PGR), which is a group of motorcycle riders and a few cages (vehicles) that ride to the airport and form a flag line to welcome home military personnel back from overseas duty. Some are in body bags, some are not. The flag line is a way of standing for those who stood for us. We also stand at funerals sometimes escorting the funeral procession to their final resting place. The PGR are all volunteers, mostly veterans who are very respectful of the PGR duties toward their fellow veterans. They were started in 2005 when an American Legion Rider's wife learned that a group of protesters disrupted a soldier's funeral. The PGR would shield families of fallen heroes from those that would disrupt the services of their loved ones, the PGR have grown to include thousands of members across all 50 states in the US.

2014

It is 2014 and almost a year since I retired from the State. I went on my first-ever Sea Cruise. Let's start by saying this was the first extensive trip Kitten and I took together. Sure, we'd been to Lake Tahoe, Colorado, and up the coast in the Redwoods, but this was our most extensive one to date. The trip started with us having to reschedule our flight to depart from Sacramena to Houston to depart from San Francisco to Houston on a Friday at 0500.

When we got to the San Francisco airport, we are told that the flight was canceled because of bad weather on the East Coast. We had to inform them that we were scheduled to go on a cruise leaving Houston that following Saturday morning. That got us a rescheduled flight to Los Angeles then to Houston by that late evening. We finally departed San Francisco at 5:30 that evening headed for LA. When we got to LA, we were rescheduled again for a later flight to Houston because of the bad East Coast weather.

We finally boarded the Cruise ship, got settled in, and were off on our voyage.

The first stop was in Cozumel, Mexico. We wanted to snorkel and visit the Aztec Ruins, then shop. We were told that with bad weather coming in we should go straight to the beach and then come back to shop. That was the best advice we received. We got to snorkel for an hour and lie on the beach for another hour and shop. By the time we got back to the port area, it started to rain very heavily. We ate, drank, and shopped then went back to the ship.

The second stop was supposed to be on the Island of Roatan, Honduras for some of the world's best snorkeling, another Mayan ruin, and shopping. The weather was so bad we just skipped the Roatan Island and went straight for Belize. On our way to Belize, the ship got infested with a Nile Virus and over 200 passengers started to get ill. The virus was a heavy dose of the flu. Luckily, neither of us caught it. The ship was unsteady with the storm, so passengers were getting seasick and with the virus on board, we were all very cautious not to touch anything.

The third stop was in the City of Belize, Belize. We were to snorkel, visit a Mayan ruin, zip line, and do some cave tubing. Again, because of the weather, we were only able to visit a ruin, shop, drink, and eat.

Then when we got back to Houston we were told we could not dock because of the fog and we would be behind the scheduled docking for over six hours, which meant we had to reschedule our departure flight out of Houston. To make a very long story short, we finally scheduled a flight from Houston to Tucson, Arizona, then to Oakland, California. We took what we could and as soon as we landed in Oakland, we rented a vehicle and drove back to Sacramena, CA. Arriving home at 1:30am that Sunday morning. Needless to say, it will be a long time before I go on a cruise again. All in all, Kitten and I made a pact before we left for this adventure that no matter what happened, we would stay positive and have fun, which is what we did.

May of 2014 my sister Gina's daughter Mesha is murdered. I've always remembered when she was a child running up to meet me whenever I visited Gina. Even as she got older and I would visit Gina, Mesha who lived two blocks over would stop whatever she was doing to greet me with a hug and a kiss. Mesha was a gifted seamstress and designer. Mesha had a gift for teaching other people via the internet how to sew and feel beautiful about their sizes. She made a great living for her children and brother who was her assistant. Mesha was an Angel to everyone who met her. She is beautiful, intelligent, driven by her family roots and children. It took her being murdered to get to know her better. Her second child's father married, abused, then divorced and stalked her and her children. Finally, Mesha moved closed to her Mom and family, only to be followed by the murderer. He snuck into her house after midnight through the back door and shot gunned her in the face in her bed as she slept next to her youngest child. It was afterwards that I finally was introduced to all that Mesha was.

Mesha's funeral was filled with family from all over the United States. I was very surprised to finally meet my biological brother Ant and Sister Kat, both on our Mom's side. I also met my Uncle Emilio and his daughter and a cousin all on Mom's side of the family. I have kept in touch with them all and especially Uncle Emilio, he and I are so much alike. I really enjoy hanging out with him. My brother is a good father and husband. The sister is kind of a lost child, she needs to take care of herself and not depend on anyone.

The last 7 years were very good to me and bad, mostly good. Now that I'm retired I have many thoughts on what I should, could, or would like to do. Plan A was to buy some property in the Redwoods overlooking the Ocean. Now there is a new Plan A, that is to move to Hawaii, Plan B, is the Redwoods. Plan C varies from San Diego, Puerto Rico, or Belize. Either way, I have to move from Sacramena and enjoy what the world has to offer. This I have to do before I am a Grandpapa. Then I will want to be a fulltime Grandpapa and very close to my Grandchild.

The people from the United States Fight League (USFL) have recruited me as a Trainer for their Athletic Inspectors. The USFL is an amateur mixed martial arts (MMA) league for children 6 years old through 18 years old. They teach young MMA fighters the rules, sportsmanship, and what the judges are looking for in wins. It is a very respectable league for young fighters. I'm still training fighters and conducting cornerman classes. I've also gone full circle and have been cornering a few amateur fighters from our gymnasium.

Today's date is Saturday January 10, 2015. I'm single again having split-up with Kitten on October 2, 2014. I had to walk away from her and our home on 10th Avenue. I only took my clothes, my biography, pictures and a few personal items. Earlier that year I had already sold the Harleys, except for the Road King. That was the first thing I sold when I moved by the river in these apartments. I feel comfortable here, I just had to get used to the apartment living. Not too private since you have people living on top, and to the sides, with thin walls and ceiling. Other than that, I feel pretty secure since it is a gated community. My side of how we split is as follows. I believe our drinking which become a more frequent thing was one of the reasons we argued. The fights got worse as we continued drinking. I tried to warn Kitten more than once that I do not like to argue, especially if we are drinking. It is not fun, and she holds a grudge for too long. When we decide to pick up her youngest son Kyle from prison we both agree on letting him live with us until he can get on his own two feet. Both of Kittens kids go with us on the trip way down south to Kyle's prison. The night before we stay a few hundred miles away in Palm Springs. We have a solid plan for the trip which her oldest does not like. We have a great time getting there except for her oldest son that is always late and bitching about one thing or another. We all share a room and her son wants to stay up and watch TV. We argue after his mother and sister complain that the TV is too loud and that we have to get up early. Finally, I tell him to turn the Fucking TV off or I'm going to throw it through the window! He gives me the stink eye, turns off the TV, throws down the remote, and packs his back pack and storms out for the night. The next morning, he is nowhere to be found. I go looking for him, I find him and apologize and ask him if he is hungry and that we will be leaving in a few to eat and get back on the road. He says that he is not hungry and that he will wait for us down in the lobby where I found him. When we meet up he whispers in his mom's ear that he does not want to talk to her for the remainder of the trip. When we pick up Kyle, I have to wake up the oldest. All the way home (6+ hours) the oldest is a prick and we can feel it in the vehicle. The next few months with Kyle in the house are going from good to bad, to worse. I know I am set in my ways but for a grown man to shower 3 times a day and shave his body while showering for up to a half hour each time is aggravating to me especially since California is in a drought situation. He doesn't want to vigorously look for a job. He thinks that he can get back into the MMA world and make money. I'm finally fed up with his trying to stay in bed till 10:00am, run around in his chones (underwear) during the day and night. I say trying because I put a stop to that twice. And getting up early (before 7:00am) just to eat and go back to bed. His uncle offers him a job in the construction field if he can get a driver's license. I purchase a couple of bicycles for him to get around since he cannot get his driver's license until he pays a $1000 fine he had before he went in. Finally, I do what I can to get him out of the house buy paying his $1000 fine, helping him with his workout by taking him to a friend's jui jitsu classes and me teaching him the boxing. He still does not talk with his uncle and the tension in the house is getting worse. I finally have a man to man talk with him that he does not like. He storms out of the house then Kitten and I argue. I gave her a choice to stay or I leave. She chooses to stay. After a few days my neighbor and I get into the house and pack what I need. I leave everything to her except for the few essential I need to cook, sleep, and clean.

The last few months of 2014 I was very fortunate. I took care of the bills, transferred my mailing, the cable, the internet, and other things that must be accomplished whenever you break up with a person you've been with for over 5+ years. Including taking her off most of the bills shared. There were a lot of penalties for the early cancellations that I had to take care of. I believe I left her much better off than when we first got together. My long-time neighbors thought I should have made her leave since it was originally my place. I just put her on the lease a few months earlier for insurance reasons. I did not agree, even though my landlord and friend thought the same thing and everyone else that knew the story. Either way, I'm coping with the burden and still saving for the great trip to Hawaii. Until I get a Driving Under the Influence (DUI) on January 1, 2015 at 11:58pm.

2015

To start the New Year, I have a very Significant Emotional Event happen to me. New Year's Eve I stay home and relax, hardly drink and enjoy the end of the year. The next day I decide to go for a short ride to air myself out, it's about 7:00pm. I end up in Old Folsom, stop and have a drink with my meal then walk around the small town. I decide to head back to town, I end up at the XO Club where I meet an old friend and his girlfriend. We have a few drinks and head towards Old Sacramena. They are not driving so they are with me. The next thing you know they are wanting to go towards West Side and home. We get to West Side and hit one more bar and they get into an argument. I decide to send them home in a taxi and I drive home. Going through Central and close to getting out

I notice a SUV vehicle come up behind me very fast. I'm guessing it's one of those Central Boys I've heard of (gang bangers and trouble makers). So, I decide to speed up and go over the black bridge towards Sacramena. By the time I clear the bridge and I'm on the Sacramena side there's another vehicle behind the SUV then I see the blue, and reds lights on me. It's the Central cops pulling me over. I know I am drunk and just go with the flow. I'm handcuffed, placed in the back of the squad car and taken to the Central County jail for the next 12 hours. They place me in the holding area where the not so violent offenders are. It is very cold, and you have to sit on hard seats, facing the front of the room away from the officers behind you in a cage. They feed you a baloney sandwich in the morning along with an apple. They do not talk to you and you do not talk to anyone either, just stare at the wall in front of you. After the 12 hours I'm released and have them call a cab for me. The cab takes me to my vehicle that is not where I left it, it was towed by the Shell gas station owners for being there overnight. The cab takes me home at a cost of $68 dollars. I'm able to get the tow companies number. I call my friend Angel and explain what happened. Luckily, she went through this a few years earlier with another friend and knew what to do and what to expect. It cost $385 to get my vehicle released. I really don't want to get into the details at this time, the wounds are still too fresh. But I do want to say that I am being proactive and have been to Alcohol Anonymous classes, Dept. of Motor Vehicles, DUI classes, Mothers Against Drunk Drivers (MADD) classes. Since talking with my lawyer because the court date is not until April 2, 2015. So far the cost is over $2500.00 and counting.

On a brighter side of this year, I'm getting prepared for Hawaii in May then the big move in August.

January, I prepared for the DUI classes and have started attending them already. I can still drive until February when I have a Hard 30-day suspension of no driving. I purchase my Regional Transit (RT) pass for the month of February, prep my bicycle, log on the Uber taxi service, start my May Hawaii schedule after talking with Howard and Lucille (they are the people whose home I will be staying in when in Hawaii's Hilo area). I refurbish my computer.

February, Adjust to RT schedule, continue classes, put vehicle in consignment dealer for month, update resume, complete taxes and pay and send for refund. Estimate cost to ship vehicle to Hilo if not sold by July. Check housing cost and location on Craigslist Hawaii.

March, continue classes, if vehicle sold continue RT schedule.

April, continue classes, court on 2nd lawyer will represent me, if vehicle sold continue RT.

May, completed classes, maybe discontinue RT, final preparations for trip on 23rd. Made recon trip to Hilo, setup condo to lease when I return in August.

June, purchase August flight, prep for move.

July, the great giveaway and estate sale list is made, maybe storage if vehicle is not shipped.

August, clear out apartment, prepare to move by 1st week (Friday the 7th),

August 5, 2015 I officially moved to Hilo, Hawaii. (During the beginning of Hurricane season). The first month 5 hurricanes past the big island. The next month 4 and a tropical storm. The funny thing is that the locals will still be out swimming, surfing, paddle boarding, etc.. I've acclimated to their style and do the same, since the weather is still in the high 70's and 80's. The first two days was unbearable here. The heat was in the 90's which made the humidity even higher. So I decided to buy a bicycle. It got better but not by much. Within a week I find the local Horse Shoe Pitching park and meet Uncle David. Uncle David is the person that the Horse shoe park is named after since he is the founder and builder of the park. After a few days of practicing he signs me up for the next Pitching Tournament a week away. So, for the next week I'm out there every morning at 10:00am practicing. Come tournament time I play and win third place. I decide to practice some more to get my percentage up for the next tournament. But, I get bored and decide to get into golfing since the 9-hole course is around the corner from where I live. I rent clubs for $10.00 and another $10.00 to play. I do this for a few weeks until I meet a guy named Charlie who invites me to play with him. Charlie is retired like me and we get along nicely. We decide to meet every Tuesday and Thursday at 7:00am to play (weather permitting). After a few weeks of playing Charlie lets me borrow his son's clubs to save me paying the $10.00 for renting them from the club. We find out that if we pay $40.00 at the beginning of the month we can play all day everyday if we wanted. So, that's what we did. My game started at a 36 handicap and within two months it's at a 22 handicap. What made it better is because I carry the bag of clubs on my back and cycle to the course which is 5 minutes away. Some days I will hit the driving range and putting greens others I will play 9-holes.

I've been able to rent a vehicle from across the street and visit other parts of the Big Island. The most exciting was being able to take a few friends to the Mauna Kea observatory which is 13,769 feet above sea level, the second highest next to Mount Everest. The air was thin and the Visitor Information Center at 7,000 feet made us wait a half an hour to get acclimated to the thin air and to make sure we had a 4-wheel drive vehicle to make the remaining journey up the mountain. The view was breathtaking, we were above the clouds and the air was clean and clear. This is very sacred grounds to the locals and now I know why. It was an experience I'll never forget.

That night I went alone to the Volcano National Park to witness the Lava bubbling up out of the volcano. Another experience I will never forget.

When I first thought about moving here my plan was to buy a home with at least half an acre. I wanted to raise Bees, built a hydroponic and Aquaponics garden, have a water catchment and solar panels and live off the land. Also to snorkel, paddle board, salsa dance, tap dance, play senior softball, golf and play horse shoes. So, I looked at a 5 different homes and put my bid on a few only to be too late or the house was too close to the current lava flow. I also was going to buy a vehicle but because I had to turn my Cadillac in my credit was messed up and I would have to buy a vehicle much more expensive than I wanted. So, I decide to stick with the bicycle and rent a vehicle once a month for entertainment and groceries. I walk as much as I can along with cycling.

I decided to check out the local boxing gymnasiums and to my surprise there weren't any that I would call a solid boxing gymnasium. I decided to put my application in at the University of Hawaii in Hilo since it was a neutral gymnasium and not affiliated with any of the other gymnasiums. They had me send my resume, then write a list of equipment needed and a class synopsis, along with class schedules. Their reply was that they would look into it and get back to me at another time. That was two months ago.

As you know I always say everything happens for a reason, so I'm thinking there's a reason things are not flowing the way I thought they would. Sure I'm having fun but I'm just not feeling it spiritually. I need to keep looking.

Even though my life in the beginning was crazy, I have matured into a God-fearing man and have done well for myself and those around me. My final thoughts to you are that no matter how bad you might begin in life, you can make a difference when you are ready, willing, and have your God on your side. No matter what religion you are, you must believe in something or someone greater than yourself. I've always been the one to come to the aid of the person on the side of the road who needed their vehicle's tire fixed or who needed it pushed off the street or to the side of the road. I was also the guy who would stop an argument or fight whenever I was close to it. I've put myself in harm's way more than I can remember because I could. I was not scared or timid; knowing I was doing the right thing was all I needed to know. I have had a lot of friends and family pass since starting this biography and I keep them alive in my mind by not only praying for them but by remembering the things we did together, along with their mannerisms, their scents, laughs and smiles, and mostly their love. My life had its ups and downs and I feel very blessed to have survived it and come out a much better human being for those around me and those who have passed.

I have to say, writing about my past, start boxing at seven, having sex with girls at eight years old, drinking and smoking pot by 10, then doing heavy drugs such as acid, speed, and mushrooms by 12, being the youngest of eight, moving out at 16 years old, my amateur and professional boxing careers, buying my first house at 18, becoming a Sergeant in the Marine Corps, being a steady State employee, an adoptive and foster parent, a custom motorcycle designer and builder, published author, multiple home and business owner, and a Latin-American Hall-of-Famer have all brought me to understand more about myself and my many failures and successes as a man. There is a God and miracles do happen; you just have to listen and have faith. Plus, surround yourself with the right people and learn from them. I sort of did both, I hung with some very bad people and some very good, I've definitely learned from both.

2020 Just to catch you up in my final chapter. I moved back from Hawaii and to the Northern California Siskiyou mountains. I'm living on the shores of a lake in a very small community 8 miles from the Oregon border. I'm single and loving the outdoor live in the country. Horseback riding, learning to rope and actually joined the volunteer fire department. Fishing, boating and quit drinking and smoking pot. Just into staying healthy. As a God fearing man I believe this is my destiny..

Printed in the United States
by Baker & Taylor Publisher Services